# SUPER SKILLS

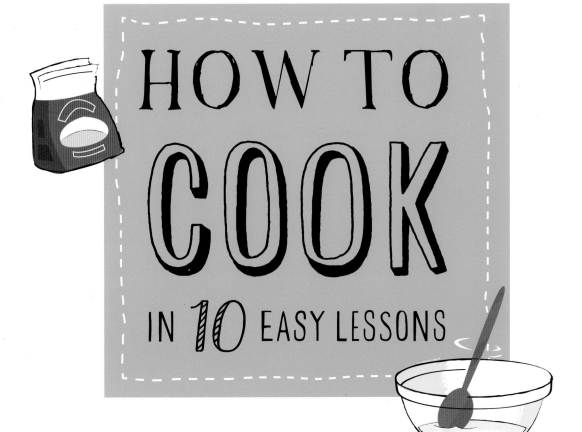

# HOW TO COOK

## IN 10 EASY LESSONS

# WENDY SWEETSER

Walter Foster
Jr.

# ABOUT THE AUTHOR

Wendy Sweetser has been a food writer for over 20 years, having trained at the Cordon Bleu culinary schools in both Paris and London. She began her career working for magazines, becoming Food Editor of Woman's Realm, TV Quick, and *OK! Magazine*. In addition to developing recipes and food styling for editorial publications, Wendy works with several large food companies developing and publicizing new products, and has written more than 25 cook books.

## PHOTO ACKNOWLEDGMENTS

The publisher thanks the following photographers and agencies for their kind permission to use their images.

All photographs by **Ian Garlick**, with the exception of the following:

**Stock food**
Pages 35, 39, 45, 56, 61.

**Shutterstock**
Pages 5, 29 (baibaz); 8 (Piotr Kreslak); 10 (Julia Metkalova); 11 (Africa Studio); 14 (MaraZe); 15 (In Tune); 20 (Maxim Pushkarev); 21 (Olga Nayashkova); 22 (MaraZ); 26 (bonchan); 28 (RoJo Images); 33 (sumire8); 34 (Martin Turzak); 38 (bonchan); 46 (Elena Veselova); 51 (minadezhda); 54 (SGM); 55 (bernashafo).

www.walterfoster.com
6 Orchard Road, Suite 100
Lake Forest, CA 92630

© Marshall Editions 2015
First published in the UK by
Marshall Editions
Part of The Quarto Group
The Old Brewery
6 Blundell Street
London N7 9BH

First published in the US by Walter Foster Jr., an imprint of Quarto Publishing Group USA Inc. All rights reserved. Walter Foster Jr. is trademarked.

Publisher: Zeta Jones
Associate Publisher: Maxime Boucknooghe
Art Director: Susi Martin
Managing Editor: Laura Knowles
Designer: Clare Barber
Original illustrations: Joanna Kerr
Principal Food Photographer: Ian Garlick

For Walter Foster:
Publisher: Anne Landa
Creative Director: Shelley Baugh
Editorial Director: Pauline Molinari
Associate Editor: Jennifer Gaudet
Copy Editors: Janessa Osle, Karen Julian
Editorial Assistant: Julie Chapa

Printed in China
1 3 5 7 9 10 8 6 4 2

# CONTENTS

# WELCOME TO THE KITCHEN!

So you want to be a super chef? It's not as difficult as you might think! All it takes is a pinch of practice, a dash of dedication, and a good splash of energy. It's one of the most useful skills you'll ever master, and you'll have a lot of fun along the way.

## ARE YOU READY?

Learning a new skill can be a little daunting, so in this book we've chopped up the subject into ten super skills you need to become a great cook. Each skill is accompanied by tasty recipes where you can try out the new techniques.

The more you cook, the more you'll enjoy it and want to experiment as you master a range of recipes. And—who knows?—what started out as a hobby could turn into your dream job when you grow up, with you as the next celebrity chef!

## BE SAFE IN THE KITCHEN

- Always wash your hands before you begin preparing food.

- Have separate chopping boards for meat, fish, and fruit and vegetables. Different colored plastic boards such as red (meat), blue (fish), and green (fruit and vegetables) make it easy to pick the right one.

- When using the stove, keep your hands far away from gas flames or hot electric rings, and be extra careful with saucepans with hot liquid.

- Arrange the oven shelves in the position you need them before turning the oven on.

- Always wear thick oven mitts when removing a hot dish from the oven.

- Don't overfill dishes or pans with sauce that could spill or boil over. Not only will spills make the oven or stove dirty, they could splash on your hands and burn them.

- Cook's knives need to be sharp for chopping and slicing ingredients, so be extra careful when using them. Keep your fingers out of the way!

**BE SAFE!**
MAKE SURE THERE IS AN ADULT NEARBY TO HELP YOU BE SAFE, ESPECIALLY WHEN USING SHARP KNIVES, A KETTLE, OR THE OVEN.

# MAKING LIFE EASIER FOR YOURSELF

- Always read a recipe all the way through before you begin.

- Get out the ingredients and measure the quantities you need.

- Decide what equipment you need to make your recipe and get these out before you begin.

- Do initial preparation like chopping onions and carrots, peeling potatoes, and trimming fat from meat before you start cooking.

- Keep your work surface tidy as you go along by clearing up peelings and returning butter or milk to the fridge once you've finished with them.

- Put empty cans, jars, utensils, and plates you've used by the sink, ready to be washed when you've finished cooking.

- Taste your recipe as you cook—all the best chefs do! It's the only way you can check if a dish needs more sugar, a pinch of salt, or an extra squeeze of lemon juice.

## CHECK YOUR SKILLS

You'll see boxes like this one on every recipe page. If you're unsure of some of the cooking skills you need to use, you can easily find the page where the technique is explained.

## You will need

Here is a list of basic equipment you'll need to try out the recipes in this book:

Grater

Whisk (balloon or electric)

Liquidizer or blender

Food processor

Wooden and large metal spoons

Measuring cup & spoons

Ice cream scoop

Cake and bread pans
(made of metal or silicone)

Sieve and colander

Knives for chopping and slicing

Chopping boards

Can opener

Baking sheets or trays

Roasting pan

Mixing bowls in different sizes

Saucepans with lids

Frying pans

Casserole dish with a lid

Kitchen scissors

Potato masher

Scales

Vegetable peeler

Rolling pin

Baking parchment

Pastry brush

Foil, paper towels, and cling wrap

DON'T FORGET YOUR APRON, OVEN MITTS, AND TEA TOWELS!

# USING KNIVES

Learning how to use a kitchen knife correctly is not difficult, but it is an important skill for any chef to learn, and essential to avoid cutting yourself.

Always ask an adult's permission to use a knife. Make sure you are sitting comfortably at a table and that the chopping board is steady. Hold the food firmly in place, with your fingers well away from the blade. Cut slowly and steadily and, if the task is a little difficult, ask an adult to help you. Always be very careful with knives, and lay them flat and out of the way when you are not using them.

## CHOOSING THE RIGHT KNIFE

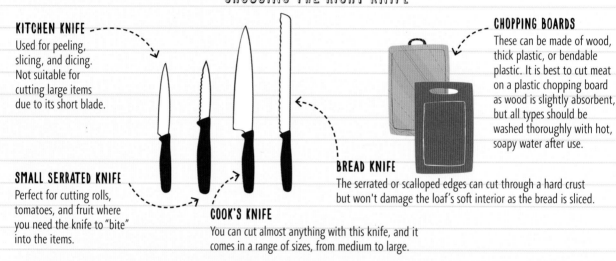

**KITCHEN KNIFE**
Used for peeling, slicing, and dicing. Not suitable for cutting large items due to its short blade.

**CHOPPING BOARDS**
These can be made of wood, thick plastic, or bendable plastic. It is best to cut meat on a plastic chopping board as wood is slightly absorbent, but all types should be washed thoroughly with hot, soapy water after use.

**SMALL SERRATED KNIFE**
Perfect for cutting rolls, tomatoes, and fruit where you need the knife to "bite" into the items.

**BREAD KNIFE**
The serrated or scalloped edges can cut through a hard crust but won't damage the loaf's soft interior as the bread is sliced.

**COOK'S KNIFE**
You can cut almost anything with this knife, and it comes in a range of sizes, from medium to large.

## Technique 1: CUTTING A TOMATO INTO WEDGES

Tomatoes are used in lots of different recipes; their vivid red color and sweet flavor makes them a popular and versatile ingredient.

1 Using a small serrated knife, carefully saw through the tomato vertically.

2 Place one half of the tomato on a board, cut side down. Cut through the rounded top, angling the knife toward the center. Repeat 2–3 times.

3 Repeat step 2 for the remaining tomato half. If you don't want to eat the seeds, scoop them out with a small spoon.

# Technique 2: SLICING AN ONION

Onions can be small or large, round or oval, and pale gold, red, or pure white in color, but they are all prepared in the same way.

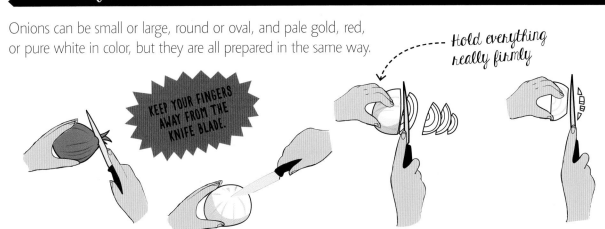

*Hold everything really firmly*

KEEP YOUR FINGERS AWAY FROM THE KNIFE BLADE.

1 Rest the onion on its side and grip it to keep it steady. Cut off the top of the onion.

2 Using the tip of the knife, peel off the onion skin and trim off the root end.

3 Hold the onion so that it is sitting on the root end. Keeping the onion steady, cut it in half, straight to the root. Turn it around and repeat on the other side to make two halves.

4 Lie one of the halves flat on the board and slice through the onion four times or more in a forward-cutting motion until you reach the center. Turn it around and repeat, holding carefully as the knife reaches the center.

5 To cut an onion into small pieces, hold a slice of onion firmly with your fingers and cut across the slice so that it forms little "cubes" of onion.

Slice up the other half of the onion in the same way.

# Technique 3: CUTTING CARROTS INTO CUBES

Like tomatoes, carrots are great for adding color and flavor to all sorts of recipes, from soups and stews to stir-fries and salads.

*try to cut pieces a similar size*

1 Peel the carrot using a vegetable peeler (see page 13) and then cut off the leafy green top and the tip of the root end.

2 Lay the carrot down on a chopping board and, holding it at the top, cut through the middle, starting at the center and cutting down to the tip. Turn the carrot around and cut through the other way from the center to the top to make two halves. Then cut each in half again lengthwise.

3 Cut across each quarter of the carrot to make small cubes, holding the thickest end of the carrot and keeping your fingers far away from the blade of the knife.

4 For carrot sticks for dipping, cut the carrot halves lengthwise, then into 1/2-inch-wide strips.

# RICH TOMATO SAUCE *for pasta*

## YOU WILL NEED

Cook's knife
Rolling pin   Chopping board
Wooden spoon   Large saucepan
Frying pan
Colander   Pepper mill

This is one of the tastiest and easiest pasta sauces to make. Serve it spooned over your favorite pasta, topped with grated Parmesan cheese.

## INGREDIENTS

- 1 onion, peeled
- 2 cloves of garlic, peeled
- 2 tbsp olive oil
- 2 x 14.5 oz cans of chopped tomatoes
- 1 tbsp tomato paste
- 1 tsp sugar
- Black pepper
- 1 handful of fresh basil leaves, chopped
- Parmesan cheese, to serve

1 Slice the onion and chop up the slices. Crush the garlic with a rolling pin or wooden spoon.

2 Heat the oil in a pan on the stove on low heat. Cook the onion for 10 minutes, adding the garlic for the last 2 minutes.

## CHECK YOUR SKILLS

- p. 7 for slicing an onion
- p. 13 for grating cheese
- p. 31 for sautéing
- p. 36 for cooking on the stove

3 Stir in the tomatoes, tomato paste, and sugar. Grind in some black pepper and stir well. Lower the heat, cover the pan with a lid, and leave to simmer gently for 15 minutes. Stir in the basil.

4 Cook your pasta according to the packet instructions. Drain, divide between 4 plates and spoon the sauce on top. Serve with a generous sprinkling of grated Parmesan cheese.

*Yummy*

**SERVES 4**

### TRY THIS!

You can use different types of pasta such as spaghetti, fusilli, or penne. Add different ingredients, such as ¼ cup chopped black olives, 4 chopped anchovy fillets, ¼ cup chopped bacon fried with the onion, or a pinch of dried chilli flakes. You could also use fresh tomatoes instead of canned.

# MINESTRONE *Soup*

Hearty soups, like this very popular one from Italy, are often described as "knife and fork soups" since they are thick, chunky, and a meal in themselves.

## INGREDIENTS

- 1 tbsp olive oil
- 1 onion, peeled and sliced
- 2 carrots, peeled and chopped
- 3 sticks of celery, chopped
- 2 garlic cloves, peeled and chopped
- 14 oz can chopped tomatoes
- 2 tbsp tomato paste
- 5 cups chicken or vegetable stock, made with stock cubes
- 14 oz can cannellini beans, drained and rinsed under cold water
- 3½ oz spaghetti, broken into shorter lengths

YOU WILL NEED

Cook's knife
Chopping board
Colander
Large saucepan with a lid
Large spoon

1 Heat the oil in a large saucepan and cook the onion and carrots over a low heat for about 10 minutes, stirring occasionally with a large spoon until the vegetables have softened.

2 Add the celery and garlic, fry for 1 minute, and then stir in the chopped tomatoes, tomato paste, and stock.

**CHECK YOUR SKILLS**

- p. 7 for slicing onions
- p. 7 for chopping carrots
- p. 31 for frying and sautéing
- p. 36 for boiling

3 Bring to a boil, and reduce the heat to a simmer. Put a lid on the saucepan and simmer the soup for 15 minutes.

5 Ladle the minestrone into soup bowls and serve with bread.

4 Add the cannellini beans and spaghetti and simmer for an additional 10 minutes or until the pasta is tender.

**TRY THIS!**
The Italians like topping this soup with grated Parmesan, sprinkling the cheese over the soup after it has been spooned into bowls.

SERVES 6

# VEGETABLE PLATTER

## YOU WILL NEED

Cook's knife

Chopping board

Colander

Kitchen towels

Serving platter

Raw vegetables cut into sticks and arranged on a large platter are known as *crudités* and they make a very colorful and tasty snack to serve at parties. Serve with a bowl of dip, such as guacamole or hummus (see recipes on pages 26 and 27).

## INGREDIENTS

- ½ cucumber
- 1 red pepper
- 1 green pepper
- 1 carrot
- 3 sticks of celery

BE CAREFUL WHEN USING A SHARP KNIFE.

## CHECK YOUR SKILLS

- p. 6–7 for choosing the right knife and slicing vegetables

1 Cut the cucumber into quarters lengthwise. You can remove the seeds or leave them in as you prefer. Cut each quarter into 3–4-inch lengths and then slice each piece into thin sticks.

2 Slice the peppers into quarters lengthwise. Cut away the stalks and the membranes inside with the seeds attached to them. Put the peppers in a colander and run cold water over them to wash away any remaining seeds. Pat the peppers dry on paper towels and cut each quarter lengthwise into sticks the same size as the cucumber.

### TRY THIS!

In addition to cucumber, peppers, carrots, and celery, you can also add whole radishes, button mushrooms, and tiny cauliflower florets to your vegetable platter.

3 Cut off any leaves at the top of the celery and pull away the loose "strings" running down the sticks, as these will be unpleasant to eat. Cut the sticks into 3–4-inch lengths and then slice into the same size as the cucumber and peppers.

4 Cut the carrot by following steps 1 and 2 on page 7; then cut the quarters lengthwise into sticks of a similar size to your other vegetables.

5 Arrange the vegetables on a serving platter, making individual piles of the different vegetables, and serve with a dip. If not serving immediately, cover the vegetables with cling wrap to prevent them from drying out.

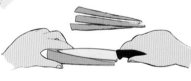

SERVES 6–8

# SUPER FRUIT SALAD

Mmm...tasty and healthy! You can use the fruits suggested here or, if you prefer, choose a selection of your favorite ones. The more colorful the combination of different fruits, the better your fruit salad will look.

## INGREDIENTS

- ½ cup apple juice
- 1 cantaloupe melon
- 2 kiwis
- 2 pineapple slices
- 2 cups strawberries
- 1 cup blueberries

## CHECK YOUR SKILLS

- p. 6 for choosing the right knives to chop, peel, and slice

## YOU WILL NEED

Measuring jug  Chopping board  Cook's knife  Kitchen knife  Large spoon  Glass serving bowl

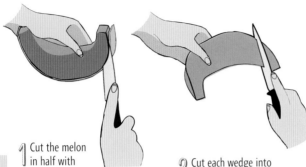

**QUICK TIP...**It's hard work to peel and chop up a whole pineapple. Unless you want to make a really big fruit salad to feed lots of people, it's easier to buy prepared slices or canned pineapple.

1 Cut the melon in half with a cook's knife, then scoop out the seeds with a spoon and discard them. Cut each half into four wedges and peel by sliding the knife around each wedge between the flesh and the rind. Cut the flesh into bite-size pieces.

2 Cut each wedge into bite-size pieces, holding the wedge steady on your chopping board and keeping your fingers out of the way of the knife.

3 Chop the pineapple slices into bite-size pieces.

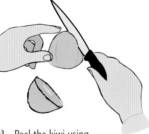

4 Peel the kiwi using a small kitchen knife. Lay the fruit on its side and cut into chunks.

5 Pull the hulls off the strawberries and cut into halves or quarters.

*so delicious*

5 Put all of the prepared fruit, plus the blueberries, into a glass bowl and pour the apple juice over the fruit. Cover the bowl with cling wrap and chill until ready to serve.

**SERVES 6–8**

# PEELING & GRATING

Peelers and graters are both important tools in a cook's kitchen, as they can be used to perform lots of different tasks. A peeler removes the skin quickly and easily from cucumbers, apples, and pears, as well as root vegetables such as potatoes, turnips, and parsnips. A grater can be used to shred hard cheese and vegetables such as carrots and zucchini, or to remove the zest from citrus fruits.

## TYPES OF PEELERS AND GRATERS

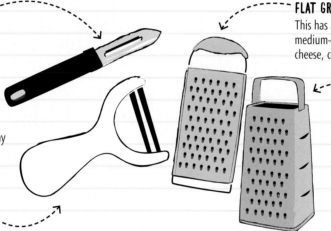

**FIXED-BLADE VEGETABLE PEELER**
Hold the non-slip handle and draw the cutting blade of the peeler over a fruit or vegetable to remove the skin in thin, even strips.

**SWIVEL-BLADE PEELER**
Can be used in the same way as a fixed-blade peeler, but shaving off long, thin slices of a vegetable is easier. The swivel blade makes it suitable for both left- and right-handed cooks.

**FLAT GRATER**
This has a single grating surface with medium-size "teeth" for grating hard cheese, chocolate, and vegetables.

**BOX GRATER**
As its name suggests, this grater is shaped like a tall box with a handle on top to hold it steady. It has a different type of grating surface on each side (e.g. a medium-grade for cheese and a fine one for citrus fruit zest.

## Technique 1: PEELING A CUCUMBER

When peeling any kind of vegetable or fruit, it's important to just remove the thin, outer layer of skin so that none of the flesh is cut away and wasted.

1 Cut the cucumber in half or quarters or leave whole, depending on how much you need for your recipe.

2 Holding the cucumber at one end, draw the cutting blade of the peeler over the skin to shave off a long, thin strip.

3 Continue around the cucumber, peeling off the skin in strips until it has all been removed.

## Technique 2: GRATING CHEESE WITH A BOX GRATER

You can only grate firm cheeses such as cheddar and Parmesan. Soft, creamy cheeses will crumble and block up the teeth of the grater.

 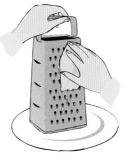  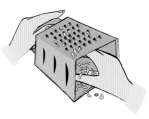

1 Hold the grater upright over a plate or bowl with one hand.

2 With the other hand, rub a block of cheese down the grating surface—make sure your fingers are kept away from the teeth as they are very sharp.

3 Hold the grater as steady as you can so that, as the cheese is grated, the flakes are collected on the plate or inside the grater.

4 Reach inside the grater to remove any cheese stuck there. Shake the grater to remove any pieces of cheese from the outside.

## Technique 3: GRATING FRUIT ZEST WITH A BOX GRATER

When lemon, lime, or orange rind needs to be added to a recipe, use the finest surface of a grater. Only grate the colorful outer zest and leave behind the white pith, which has a bitter taste. If you can, use unwaxed fruit.

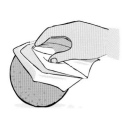   

1 Wash the fruit in warm water and dry with a paper towel.

2 Stand the grater upright on a plate and steady it by holding the handle on top.

3 Keeping the fruit whole, rub the skin over the finest surface of the grater to remove the zest, grating until the white pith is just visible and turning the fruit as you go.

4 When all the zest has been removed, use a brush to remove any still clinging to the teeth of the grater. Don't try to remove it using your fingers, since you could cut yourself on the sharp teeth.

# PORK KEBABS with Mint & Cucumber Yogurt Dip

## YOU WILL NEED

Cook's knife
Chopping board
Spoon
Grater
Fork
8–12 metal or wooden skewers
Pastry brush
Mixing bowl

Kebabs are fun to eat, and marinating the meat before you thread it onto the skewers gives the kebabs extra flavor. They go perfectly with a cool mint & cucumber yogurt dip, known as "raita" in India, where it is served with spicy curries.

## INGREDIENTS

### FOR THE KEBABS:
- 1 lb 2 oz lean pork loin steaks
- 2 tbsp olive oil
- 2 tbsp orange juice
- 1 tbsp clear honey
- 1 red pepper
- 2 zucchinis

### FOR THE DIP:
- ¾ cup thick Greek yogurt
- 8 fresh mint leaves, finely chopped
- ¼ cucumber, peeled and grated

## CHECK YOUR SKILLS
- p. 6 for using knives
- p. 12 for peeling
- p. 42 for grilling

- p. 6 for using knives
- p. 12 for peeling
- p. 42 for grilling

### TRY THIS!
When the weather is warm outside, you can grill the kebabs on a barbecue. Experiment by trying out different types of meat and vegetables on your kebabs.

1 Trim any fat from the pork steaks and cut the meat into 1-inch cubes.

2 Put the olive oil, orange juice, and honey into a mixing bowl and whisk the ingredients together with a fork until evenly combined.

3 Cut the pepper in half and deseed it, then cut it into 1-inch pieces. Trim off the tops and bottoms of the zucchinis and cut into bite-size pieces.

4 Add the pork and vegetables to the bowl and stir until coated with the orange and honey mixture. Leave in a cool place to marinate for 1 hour, stirring occasionally.

5 Thread the pork, pepper, and zucchini pieces alternately onto the skewers. Lay the kebabs side by side in a single layer on a grill pan—line the pan first with foil for an easy clean-up afterward!

SERVES 4

6 Preheat the grill to high and grill the kebabs for 6–7 minutes, turning them over once or twice, or until the pork is cooked and the vegetables are browned at the edges. If any marinade is left in the bowl, brush this over the kebabs as they cook.

### QUICK TIP...
If you use wooden skewers, soak them in a bowl of cold water for 30 minutes beforehand or cover the exposed ends with small pieces of aluminum foil to prevent them from burning on the grill.

7 Make the dip by putting the yogurt in a small bowl and stirring in the grated cucumber and chopped mint. Serve at once with the kebabs.

# CHEESE STRAWS

These tasty, savory breadsticks are delicious on their own as a snack or served with soup. This recipe uses a mixture of mature cheddar and Parmesan, but feel free to use other hard cheeses with strong flavors, if you prefer.

## INGREDIENTS

- 5 oz mature cheddar cheese
- ½ cup Parmesan cheese
- 3 cups plain flour, plus a little extra for dusting
- 2 sticks butter, diced
- 1 large egg, beaten

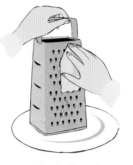

**YOU WILL NEED**

Grater
Mixing bowl
Cook's knife
Sieve
Baking sheet
Parchment
Rolling pin
Cling wrap
Fish spatula

**CHECK YOUR SKILLS**
- - - - - - - - - - - - - -
- p. 13 for grating cheese

1 Grate the cheddar and Parmesan cheeses onto a plate.

2 Sift the flour into a mixing bowl and, using your fingertips, rub in the butter until there are no lumps of butter left and the mixture looks like fine breadcrumbs. Stir in the grated cheeses, the beaten egg, and 4 tablespoons of cold water.

**QUICK TIP...**The butter will be much easier to rub into the flour if you take it out of the fridge about 30 minutes before you want to make the cheese straw dough. This will allow the butter to get to room temperature and soften a little.

**TRY THIS!**
For a spicy kick, sift 1 teaspoon of chilli powder or paprika into the mixing bowl with the flour.

3 Use your hands to bring the ingredients together to form a ball of dough, adding a little more cold water if needed. Wrap the dough in cling wrap and chill in the fridge for 30 minutes to harden it up.

4 Preheat the oven to 375°F. Dust the work surface with a little flour and roll out the dough into a square about ¼-inch thick.

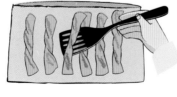

5 Cut the square in half and then cut each half into ½-inch strips. Take one strip of pastry and twist it two or three times. Carefully lift it onto the baking sheet and press the ends of the strips down lightly. Repeat with all of the remaining strips of dough and then bake them for 10–15 minutes until crisp.

6 Leave the cheese straws to cool on the baking sheet before lifting them off with a fish spatula.

**MAKES ABOUT 36**

# KEY LIME PIE

## YOU WILL NEED

*Large pitcher*

*Mixing bowl*

*Plastic bag and rolling pin or food processor*

*Balloon whisk*

*Large metal spoon*

*Saucepan*

*9-inch pie dish*
*Baking sheet*

This rich and creamy pie from Florida is traditionally made using the key limes that are native to the sunshine state. If you can't find key limes, ordinary limes will still make a delicious pie.

## INGREDIENTS

**FOR THE PIE CRUST:**
- 8 oz Graham crackers
- 8 tbsp unsalted butter

**FOR THE PIE FILLING:**
- 14 oz can sweetened condensed milk
- 4 egg yolks
- 1 cup heavy cream
- finely grated zest of 2 limes
- ½ cup freshly squeezed lime juice

1 To make the pie crust, preheat the oven to 400° F. Crush the crackers to crumbs either in a plastic bag using a rolling pin or in a food processor. Transfer the crumbs to a mixing bowl.

2 Melt the butter in a saucepan over low heat and pour it into the cracker crumbs. Mix well and then spoon the crumbs into the pie dish, pressing them down firmly with the back of the spoon so that they cover the base and come up the sides of the plate.

## CHECK YOUR SKILLS

- p. 13 for grating citrus zest
- p. 19 for juicing citrus fruit
- p. 19 for crushing cookies
- p. 42–43 for using the oven

3 Put the pie dish on a baking sheet, bake the crust for 10 minutes, and then remove it from the oven. Lower the oven temperature to 325° F.

4 To make the filling, put the condensed milk in a large jug, add the egg yolks, and whisk together until combined. Stir in the heavy cream, lime zest, and lime juice.

5 Carefully pour the filling into the cooked crust and bake the pie for 15 minutes.

6 Allow the pie to cool completely and then chill it in the fridge for 2–3 hours before serving.

## TRY THIS!
Cut the pie into wedges to serve, topping each serving with a spoonful of whipped cream and a fresh lime wedge.

SERVES 8

**QUICK TIP...** It is easiest to squeeze the juice out of limes if you soften them first. Grate the zest off the limes and then put them in the microwave and give them a 5-second zap on full power.

# APPLE TARTS

These tarts make a really impressive dessert, especially if you serve them with whipped cream or scoops of vanilla ice cream. Make one large tart and cut it into individual portions before serving.

## INGREDIENTS

- 1 sheet of ready-rolled puff pastry
- 1 egg, beaten
- 3 tbsp ground almonds
- 3 tbsp sugar
- 3 dessert apples
- 2 tbsp unsalted butter
- 3 tbsp apricot jam
- 3 tbsp chopped almonds

## YOU WILL NEED

Baking sheet

Cook's knife

Pastry brush

Chopping board

Saucepan

1 Unwrap the pastry and lay it on a baking sheet. Brush the top of the pastry all over with the beaten egg to glaze.

2 Mix the ground almonds with 1 tablespoon of the sugar and scatter over the pastry. With a knife, score the pastry into six equal pieces, without cutting all the way through the pastry.

## CHECK YOUR SKILLS

- p. 6 for using knives
- p. 12 for peeling
- p. 42–43 for using the oven

3 Peel the apples, cut into quarters, and remove the cores. Slice each quarter lengthwise into thin slices.

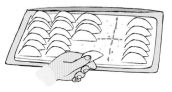

4 Arrange the apple slices over the pastry, between the score lines. Scatter the remaining sugar over the apples.

5 Cut up the butter into small pieces and dot over the apples. Preheat the oven to 400°F and bake for 25–30 minutes or until the pastry is puffed and golden brown and the apples are soft.

6 Warm the apricot jam in a small saucepan over low heat and brush the jam over the apples. Scatter the chopped almonds on top. Cut the tart into portions along the scored lines and serve warm.

**QUICK TIP...**When brushing the pastry with beaten egg, be careful not to let the egg run down the sides of the pastry. If this happens, the layers in the pastry will stick together and won't rise up and become beautifully crisp and flaky in the oven.

*Delicious...*

SERVES 6

### TRY THIS!
You can also make the tarts using shortcrust pastry if you prefer. If using a block of pastry, roll it out on a board dusted with flour to a rectangle measuring about 8 x 12 inches—trim the edges with a cook's knife to make them neat. Top with the almonds and apples and bake in an oven 350°F for 45 minutes.

# CRUSHING & JUICING

A food processor is useful for taking the hard work out of lots of kitchen jobs, such as making breadcrumbs or mincing meat. However, many tasks, such as crushing Graham crackers to make crumbs for the base of a cheesecake, are easy to do by hand and you don't need any special equipment.

## THE FOOD PROCESSOR

Food processors do lots of tasks, from chopping and slicing to mixing, puréeing, blending, and grating.

The ingredients to be processed are put straight in the machine's bowl, with the cutting or mixing attachment fitted. Once the lid of the bowl has been clipped firmly in place, the motor is switched on and the food is mixed or chopped. Alternatively, the ingredients can be pushed or fed down the upright tube attached to the lid with the motor running. This method is used when you are slicing or grating cheese or vegetables, such as carrots and zucchinis. It can also be used for adding a liquid gradually to a pastry or bread dough or a dressing, such as mayonnaise.

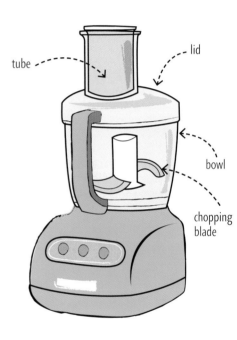

tube — lid — bowl — chopping blade

## TYPES OF JUICERS

this is a handy piece of equipment to have in your kitchen.

### JUICE EXTRACTOR
You can use this type of machine to extract juice from lots of different fruits and vegetables, such as mangos or carrots.

### SIMPLE CITRUS JUICE PRESS
This is a shallow-sided dish that has a ridged dome in the center on top. It is very easy to use to squeeze the juice from citrus fruits such as lemons, small oranges, and limes.

### HAND-CRANKED CITRUS JUICE PRESS
These are larger machines designed to extract the juice from big oranges, grapefruits, and pomelos.

# Technique 1: MAKING BREAD CRUMBS

Add the bread to the food processor one piece at a time so that they are reduced evenly to crumbs. You can also make biscuit crumbs in the same way.

ASK AN ADULT TO HELP YOU WHEN HANDLING A FOOD PROCESSOR BLADE.

1 Weigh out the quantity of bread you need. It's best to use bread that is a few days old, once it has become a little dry.

2 Place the bowl in position on the food processor, fit with the double-sided chopping blade, and clip the lid on top.

3 With the motor running, drop the pieces of bread down the feeder tube until all the bread has been added and chopped into evenly sized crumbs.

4 Transfer the crumbs to a bowl, scraping out any pieces that are trapped in the corners of the food processor's bowl.

# Technique 2: CRUSHING COOKIES BY HAND

Do this on a hard surface such as a chopping board. Seal the bag so that the crumbs don't shoot out of the top, and hold the bag steady, making sure you keep your hand away from the rolling pin!

1 Put the cookies in a large or medium-sized freezer bag and push out most of the air before you seal it, in case the bag bursts when you hit it with the rolling pin.

2 Put the bag of cookies on a chopping board. Hold the bag with your hand so it doesn't move around on the board as you make the crumbs.

3 Smash the cookies in the bag with a rolling pin to break them into small pieces. Continue to smash the cookies until they are reduced to crumbs. Open the bag and tip the crumbs into a bowl.

# Technique 3: JUICING A CITRUS FRUIT

When using a juice press, the juice either collects in the dish around the dome or the dish will have draining holes and sit above a bowl for the juice to flow into.

1 If using a simple citrus juice press, cut small citrus fruit, such as a lemon, lime, or orange in half through the center.

2 Put half the fruit, cut side down, over the dome and press down firmly, twisting the fruit as you press to extract the juice.

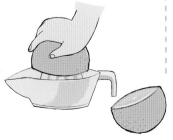

1 If using a hand-cranked citrus juice press, put halves of fruit cut side down in the press.

2 Pull down the handle or turn it, depending on the style of machine you are using. The juice that runs out collects in the pitcher or bowl that comes with the machine.

# HOMEMADE FISH STICKS

## YOU WILL NEED
Food processor
2 large plates and
1 shallow bowl
Cook's knife
Fish spatula
Chopping board    Fork
Large frying pan
Paper towels

Want to make fish sticks from scratch? It's super easy. You can use any firm white fish, but thicker fillets, such as cod or haddock work better than flat fish, such as plaice or sole.

## INGREDIENTS
- 1 lb thick white fish fillets
- 6 slices of stale white bread, crusts removed
- 4 tbsp plain flour
- 1 egg
- oil for shallow frying

1 Place the fish fillets skin side down on a chopping board. Using a cook's knife, work the blade between the skin and the flesh of the fish at the tail end of the fillet to loosen it. Holding the knife with the blade away from you and at a

45 degree angle, move the blade backward and forward down the fillet so the flesh comes away from the skin in a single piece. Repeat with the remaining fillets and cut the flesh into 1-inch sticks across the grain of the flesh.

## CHECK YOUR SKILLS
- p. 6 for using knives
- p. 19 for using a food processor
- p. 30 for shallow frying

2 Tear up the bread slices into smaller pieces and drop in the food processor bowl. Process for about 30 seconds, or until completely crumbled. Pour out the crumbs onto a large plate and spread out the flour on another plate.

**TRY THIS!**
Mix the bread crumbs with 1 teaspoon of dried thyme or 1/2 teaspoon of a spice such as paprika or ground coriander before coating the fish.

3 Crack the egg into a shallow bowl and beat lightly with a fork.

4 Coat the fish sticks with flour and then with the beaten egg before putting them on the plate and patting the crumbs all over them. Chill the sticks until you are ready to cook them.

5 Heat about 4 tablespoons of oil in a large frying pan, add the crumbled fish sticks, and fry over medium heat for 5–6 minutes or until golden, turning over occasionally so they cook evenly. Remove from the pan with a fish spatula and place on a plate lined with paper towels.

**SERVES 4**

**QUICK TIP...** Use an oil with a neutral flavor to fry the fish sticks, such as sunflower, grapeseed, or groundnut oil.

6 Serve the fish sticks while they're hot, with lemon wedges to squeeze over them and tartar sauce or ketchup.

# MEATBALLS *in Tomato Sauce*

You can serve these tasty meatballs with mashed potatoes and vegetables or spoon them over pasta. You can prepare the meatballs ahead of time and chill them in the fridge on a plate covered in cling wrap until you are ready to cook them.

**YOU WILL NEED**

Large spoon

Cook's knife

Large bowl

Spatula

Frying pan

## INGREDIENTS

**FOR THE MEATBALLS:**
- 4 tbsp olive oil
- 1 small onion, peeled and chopped as finely as you can
- 1 lb ground lean beef
- ½ cup breadcrumbs (see Fish Sticks recipe, page 20)
- 1 egg, beaten
- Ground black pepper
- A little plain flour, for dusting

**FOR THE TOMATO SAUCE:**
- 1 quantity of rich tomato sauce for spaghetti (see page 8)

1 Heat 1 tablespoon of the olive oil in a frying pan over gentle heat. Add the chopped onion, cover the pan, and cook for about 5 minutes until the onion is soft and turning golden. Remove the onion from the pan and set aside to cool.

2 In a large bowl, mix together the ground beef, bread crumbs, and cold cooked onion, breaking up any lumps of meat with a spoon.

3 Stir in the beaten egg and season with lots of ground black pepper.

**CHECK YOUR SKILLS**
- p. 7 for chopping onions
- p. 8 for making tomato sauce
- p. 30–31 for frying and sautéing

**QUICK TIP...** The meatballs can be made with lean lamb or pork if you prefer.

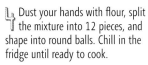

4 Dust your hands with flour, split the mixture into 12 pieces, and shape into round balls. Chill in the fridge until ready to cook.

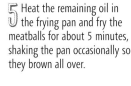

5 Heat the remaining oil in the frying pan and fry the meatballs for about 5 minutes, shaking the pan occasionally so they brown all over.

**TRY THIS!**
When cooked, spoon the meatballs and tomato sauce into a shallow oven-proof dish, top with ½ cup of grated mozzarella cheese, and place under a hot grill until the cheese melts and bubbles.

6 Spoon out any excess oil from the frying pan before pouring the tomato sauce over the meatballs. Bring the sauce to a boil, lower the heat under the pan, and simmer for 15 minutes. Serve hot with mashed potatoes and vegetables or spooned over pasta.

**SERVES 4**

# NEW YORK CHEESECAKE

This classic cheesecake has a buttery graham cracker base that melts in the mouth. Just the sort of dessert to make if you're trying to "butter" up your parents!

## INGREDIENTS

**FOR THE BASE:**
- 1/2 stick unsalted butter
- 7 oz graham crackers

**FOR THE TOPPING:**
- 1 cup full fat cream cheese
- 1 cup ricotta cheese
- 2/3 cup sugar
- 4 large eggs
- 1 tsp vanilla extract
- 1 1/4 cups full fat sour cream

## CHECK YOUR SKILLS

- p. 19 for crushing cookies
- p. 52 for beating

SERVES 6-8

1 To make the base, melt the butter in a saucepan, remove the pan from the heat, and stir in the graham cracker crumbs.

2 Spoon the crumbs into a 9-inch springform cake pan and press over the base with the back of the spoon. Chill in the fridge while you make the topping.

3 To make the topping, in a large bowl, beat together the cream cheese and ricotta cheese with half the sugar until evenly mixed.

4 Beat in the eggs, one at a time, followed by the vanilla.

5 Pour this mixture over the graham cracker base and stand the pan on a baking sheet.

6 Preheat the oven to 300°F and bake the cheesecake for an hour. Remove it from the oven and let it stand for 5 minutes.

7 Stir the rest of the sugar into the sour cream and pour over the cheesecake. Return it to the oven for 5 minutes, then remove the cheesecake and leave it to cool completely before removing from the pan.

*Scrumptious*

**TRY THIS!**
For a special treat, serve the cheesecake with either chocolate sauce or fruit purée drizzled over each serving. Go to pages 48 and 49 to find out how to make these scrumptious toppings.

**QUICK TIP...**Instead of vanilla, you can flavor the cheese with lemon. Stir the grated zest from 1 large or 2 small lemons into the cream cheese mixture and leave out the vanilla extract.

# FRESH LEMONADE

This lemonade is very easy to make and is the perfect summer drink for picnics on the beach or barbecues in the backyard. Add some ice cubes or crushed iced to each glass before pouring in the lemonade.

## INGREDIENTS
- 4 large, unwaxed lemons
- ½ cup sugar

TO SERVE:
- 1 liter of sparkling mineral water or soda water
- Ice cubes or crushed ice

## YOU WILL NEED
Vegetable peeler
Cook's knife
Large pitcher
Bowl
Two forks
Citrus juicer
Tall glasses, to serve

1 Using a vegetable peeler, cut away the zest from each lemon in strips, working from the top to the bottom of a lemon until it is all removed. Put the strips in a bowl.

2 Cut the zested lemons in half and squeeze the juice.

## CHECK YOUR SKILLS
- p. 12 for peeling
- p. 19 for juicing

**TRY THIS!**
To give your lemonade a pretty pink color, add a dash of grenadine to the pitcher.

3 Add the juice to the bowl along with the sugar, stirring until the sugar dissolves. Leave to stand for 30 minutes so the zest adds extra flavor to the juice.

4 With a fork, lift out the zest and discard.

*so refreshing!*

5 Pour the juice mixture into a large pitcher and top off with the mineral water or soda water. Stir to combine.

6 Fill tall glasses with ice cubes or crushed ice half way and pour in the lemonade.

**SERVES 4**

**QUICK TIP...** Be careful to just peel away the thin layer of yellow zest from the lemons and leave the bitter white pith behind.

# MASHING & PURÉEING

Have you ever tried to make mashed potatoes with a fork? It's not much fun! It's much quicker to use a real masher, as you'll get a much smoother, creamier result. It's also easy to whip up a smoothie or a soup if you have a blender. Here's all the info you need to master Super Skill 4!

## TYPES OF BLENDERS AND MASHERS

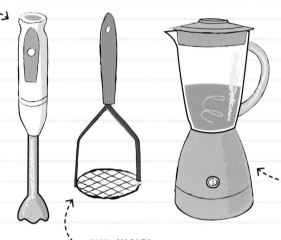

**HANDHELD BLENDER**

This handy machine is also known as an "immersion blender." It has a long, round shaft that is easy to hold in one hand, with a small, revolving blade attached to the end. Some blenders come with a beaker that can be used for blending small amounts of ingredients.

**STANDING BLENDER**

This free-standing blender is made up of a stand, which contains the motor, and a clear plastic pitcher that sits on top. The pitcher has a revolving blade at the bottom and a tight-fitting lid. When blending fruit or vegetables in a standing blender, you need to add a liquid, such as stock or fruit juice, or the blender won't work properly.

**HAND MASHER**

This is used to turn cooked vegetables, such as potatoes, carrots, turnips, parsnips, and peas, into a smooth, lump-free mash.

## Technique 1: USING A STANDING BLENDER TO BLEND SOUP

Standing blenders are mainly used for puréeing vegetables and to make soups and fruit smoothies.

1 Simmer the ingredients, such as chopped vegetables or lentils, in stock or water, until they are very tender. Leave to cool—you can burn yourself if you blend the mixture while it is still hot.

2 Snap the pitcher in place on its stand. Spoon enough of the soup mixture into the pitcher to fill it about half full.

3 Fit the lid on top and keep your hand on the lid as you blend to ensure it stays firmly in place. Turn the switch on the stand to full speed and blend the mixture until it is smooth.

4 Pour the purée into a clean saucepan, ready to be reheated. Blend the rest of the soup in the same way.

# Technique 2: USING A HANDHELD BLENDER TO PURÉE FRUIT

As well as puréeing fruit and vegetables, handheld blenders are useful for doing all sorts of kitchen jobs, such as making smoothies, whipping cream, whisking pancake batter, and making sure a gravy or sauce isn't lumpy.

1 Prepare the fruit as necessary by peeling and removing cores, pits, and stalks. Chop the flesh to be puréed into evenly sized pieces. If you are only blending a small quantity, place the fruit pieces in a blender beaker. If you are blending a larger quantity, put the fruit into a mixing bowl.

2 Plug in the blender (if necessary) and, holding it directly upright, put the blade in the fruit. Make sure the blade is completely covered by the fruit to avoid any splatters flying up while you are blending.

3 Press the on/off button on the shaft of the blender and keep the blade immersed in the fruit until it becomes a smooth purée. Switch off before lifting out the blade.

4 Use a spatula to scrape out the purée and wash the blender head in the sink.

# Technique 3: MASHING POTATOES

Before they can be mashed, the potatoes must be steamed or boiled until they are very tender—but not disintegrating. Test if they are done by piercing them with a fork. You can also mash other root vegetables.

*Make sure they're nice and soft*

1 If boiling the vegetables, drain them thoroughly when cooked and return to the saucepan. If steaming, transfer them to a dry pan.

2 Hold the masher upright and push the grid-like head into the soft vegetables.

3 Lifting the masher up and then pushing it down quite firmly, work your way around the pan until all the vegetables are crushed and reduced to a smooth mash.

3 For a tasty, creamy mash, add a pat of butter and a splash of milk while you're mashing the vegetables.

# GUACAMOLE

## YOU WILL NEED

Chopping board
Spoon
Cook's knife
Two bowls
Hand masher or fork
Handheld blender

This can be spooned onto burgers and baked potatoes, served with fajitas or tacos (see recipe on page 33), or used as a dip with tortilla chips. It is traditionally quite spicy, but you can reduce the number of chilies—or add more if you like things hot!

## INGREDIENTS

- 3 red chilies
- Small bunch of cilantro
- 2 medium tomatoes, finely chopped
- 1 small onion, peeled and finely chopped
- Juice of 2 limes
- 3 ripe avocados

### BE CAREFUL WITH CHILIES!

The heat of chilies comes from the seeds and membranes inside. They can give a nasty burning sensation if you touch your face or rub your eyes with your fingers after preparing them. To avoid this, use a fork and small, sharp knife so your fingers don't come in contact with the chilies, or wash your hands immediately afterwards.

1 Cut the stalks off the chilies and slit them open lengthwise. Scrape out the seeds and membranes and chop the flesh into fine pieces.

## CHECK YOUR SKILLS

- p. 6 for using knives
- p. 25 for puréeing and mashing

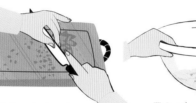

2 Coarsely chop the cilantro leaves.

*Snack time!*

3 Put the chilies, cilantro, half of the chopped tomatoes, onion, and the juice of 1 lime in a bowl and blend until you have a fine paste.

4 Cut the avocados in half lengthwise, remove the pits, and scoop out the flesh into a mixing bowl using a spoon.

**QUICK TIP...**Once avocado flesh is exposed to the air it starts to turn brown. To keep the guacamole looking nice and green, drizzle a little lemon or lime juice over the top after spooning it into a serving bowl. Then press cling wrap over the surface.

5 Mash the avocado flesh coarsely with the rest of the lime juice, using a hand masher or fork.

6 Stir in the chili paste and the rest of the tomato until evenly mixed. Spoon into a small serving bowl and chill until ready to serve.

SERVES 6

# HUMMUS

Hummus is made by blending together chickpeas, lemon juice, garlic, and a paste made from ground sesame seeds called "tahini." It is served as a dip with vegetable crudités (see recipe on page 10) or pieces of warm pita bread. Hummus originates from the Middle East, but it is now popular all over the world.

## YOU WILL NEED

Colander for rinsing the chickpeas

Cook's knife or garlic press

Large spoon

Citrus press

Standing blender or handheld blender

## INGREDIENTS

- 14 oz can chickpeas, drained and rinsed under cold water
- 3 tbsp lemon juice (or to taste)
- 3 garlic cloves, skinned and finely chopped or crushed
- 3 tbsp tahini (sesame seed paste)
- 3 tbsp water
- 1 tbsp extra virgin olive oil
- salt and pepper, to taste

TO SERVE:
- 2 tbsp extra virgin olive oil
- 1 tsp paprika

1 Put the chickpeas in a standing blender or bowl, and add the lemon juice, garlic, tahini, water, and olive oil.

2 Blend everything together until the mixture is very smooth. Taste the hummus and adjust the flavor if necessary—you may need to add a little more lemon juice. Season with a little salt and pepper as well.

## CHECK YOUR SKILLS

- p. 19 for juicing lemons
- p. 24–25 for using a standing blender or handheld blender

**QUICK TIP...** You can also scatter some toasted pine nuts over the hummus before you serve it. To toast the nuts, spread them out on a baking sheet and place in a 325 °F oven for 4–5 minutes until they are golden. Turn them over halfway through, so they toast evenly. When the nuts are ready, remove them from the baking sheet right away or they might burn.

3 Spoon the hummus into a small bowl or spread it out on a flat plate, leveling the top with the back of the spoon.

4 To serve, drizzle the olive oil over the top of the hummus and sprinkle with paprika.

SERVES 6

# TWICE BAKED POTATOES

## YOU WILL NEED

Baking tray

Mixing bowl

Cook's knife

Spoon

Hand masher

Fork

These baked potatoes are great for dinner or a party, especially if it's a cold night and everyone is hungry!

## INGREDIENTS

- 2 large potatoes
- 1 cup grated cheddar cheese
- 4 tbsp milk
- 4 oz cooked ham, cut into small pieces
- Freshly ground black pepper

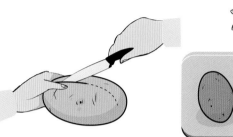

### CHECK YOUR SKILLS

- p. 6 for using knives
- p. 12 for grating cheese
- p. 25 for hand mashing
- p. 43 for baking

1 Preheat the oven to 350°F. Wash the potatoes and pat dry with paper towels. Using a sharp knife, score a line just through the skin lengthwise around the center of each potato.

2 Put the potatoes on a baking tray and bake for 1 hour or until they are tender. Push a toothpick into the center of each to see if they are ready. Leave the potatoes to cool.

**QUICK TIP...** When scooping out the potato flesh, leave about 1/8-inch of the flesh attached to the skin to support it. Be careful not to break the skins as you scoop.

3 Cut the potatoes in half along the scored lines and scoop out the flesh into a bowl with a spoon. Mash the potato flesh with a hand masher.

4 Add the milk, cheese, and ham to the mashed potatoes and stir until evenly mixed. Season with black pepper.

5 Spoon the mixture into the potato shells, pressing it down with a fork and mounding it up a little in the center. Put the potato shells back on the baking sheet and return to a 350°F oven for 30 minutes or until piping hot.

### TRY THIS!

Instead of ham, you could add other ingredients to the mashed potatoes—try cooked, chopped bacon, finely chopped green onions, or sweet corn kernels.

SERVES 4

# STRAWBERRY & BANANA SMOOTHIE

Everyone loves a cool, creamy smoothie! Once you've made one yourself, you'll never want to go back to drinking the store-bought kind.

## INGREDIENTS

- 1 banana
- 1 cup strawberries
- 1⅔ cup milk
- ½ cup strawberry or Greek yogurt

### YOU WILL NEED

Chopping board

Cook's knife

Handheld blender

Measuring cup

Large bowl

3-4 tall glasses

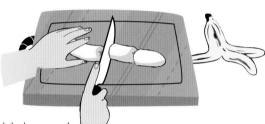

1 Peel the banana and cut it into three or four pieces.

**SERVES 3-4**

### CHECK YOUR SKILLS

- p. 6 for using knives
- p. 25 for puréeing using a handheld blender

**QUICK TIP...**On a hot day, don't forget to add a couple of ice cubes to each glass before serving, or chill the glasses in the fridge for 1 hour first.

2 Wash the strawberries and pat them dry with paper towels. Remove the green hulls and chop into halves or quarters.

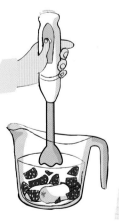

3 Put the banana and strawberries in a pitcher and add the milk and yogurt.

4 Blend until smooth. Pour into tall glasses and serve.

# FRYING, SAUTÉING & BROWNING

Frying or sautéing on the stove are quick ways to cook all kinds of foods. Different types of pans are used to fry eggs or make an omelette, fry potatoes for hash browns, sear a steak, or stir-fry chicken and vegetables for a tasty feast.

## CHOOSING THE RIGHT PAN FOR THE JOB

### FRYING PANS

Frying pans are wide pans with a flat base and shallow sides. They come in different sizes and can be made of stainless steel, with or without a non-stick coating, or cast iron. They are used on the stove to fry ingredients such as meat, fish, eggs, and vegetables in a small amount of oil. Frying can be done over a medium or high heat, depending on the recipe.

### WOKS

Chinese woks are deep pans that have a long handle and rounded base. Like frying pans, they come in a variety of sizes and are made from different materials such as carbon steel, stainless steel, and aluminum.

Woks are used for stir-frying ingredients in a tiny amount of oil over a high heat. Meat, seafood, and vegetables are first cut into small, evenly-sized pieces and then tossed continuously in a wok with a metal spatula so they cook very quickly and evenly. Other ingredients, such as rice and noodles, are pre-cooked in another pan before being added.

### WATCH OUT!

Be extra careful when cooking with hot oil. If food is dropped into the pan, the oil could splash up and burn your hand or catch fire if it comes into contact with a gas flame. Always ask an adult to help.

### SAUTÉ PANS

These are similar to frying pans but have deeper sides and a lid so ingredients, such as onions, can be softened or "sweated" over a low heat with the lid on, and then browned with the lid removed and the heat increased.

## Technique 1: FRYING SAUSAGES

When frying sausages you can add a little oil to the pan, or dry fry them without any oil if you prefer.

*Be careful when heating oil in a pan.*

1 If your sausages are linked together, snip them apart with kitchen scissors but avoid pricking the skins of the sausages with a fork as they could split when you fry them.

2 Place a frying pan on the stove over medium heat and add 1 tablespoon of a flavorless oil such as canola, sunflower, or vegetable oil.

3 When the pan is hot, carefully place the sausages in the pan one at a time, making sure they are not touching each other.

4 Cook for 8–12 minutes, depending on how large the sausages are. Turn over occasionally with tongs, or roll over by shaking the pan so that the sausages brown evenly on all sides.

# Technique 2: SAUTÉING ONIONS

Sliced or chopped onions are best cooked in a sauté pan over low heat with the lid on. This allows the onions to soften and release their sweet flavor.

1 Peel your onions and chop or cut them into thin slices (see page 7).

2 Heat a sauté pan on the stove over a low heat and add 2 tablespoons of oil. This can be a flavorless oil or it can be olive oil, which will add its own flavor to the onions as they cook.

3 Add the chopped onions, put the lid on the pan, and sauté the onions over a low heat for about 15–20 minutes until they are really soft but haven't turned brown.

4 Take the lid off the pan and stir the onions occasionally with a large spoon or spatula so they soften evenly.

5 Once the onions are soft, remove the lid and raise the heat to medium. Cook for an additional 5–10 minutes until the onions are golden brown, stirring them frequently so they don't stick to the bottom of the pan and burn.

# Technique 3: BROWNING BEEF

When making a casserole, you need to brown the pieces of meat in hot oil first so that they become caramelized and all their flavor and juices are sealed in. This can be done in a sauté pan (without the lid on) or in the casserole dish you are using, as long as it is flameproof—such as one made of stainless steel or cast iron—and suitable to go on the stove as well as in the oven.

   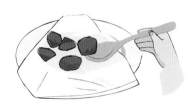

1 Trim any fat from your meat —this can be beef, pork, or lamb—and, using a large cook's knife, cut the meat into 1-inch cubes. Wash your hands.

WASH YOUR HANDS AFTER HANDLING RAW MEAT.

2 Put the pan on the stove over high heat and add 1 tablespoon of a flavorless oil.

3 When the oil is hot, add five or six pieces of meat to the pan, using a large spoon and wearing an oven mitt, since the cold meat could make the hot oil spit.

4 Stir the meat occasionally so the pieces brown on all sides. Lift them out with the spoon and transfer to a plate. Repeat with the remaining pieces. If the pan becomes dry, add a little more oil to stop the meat from sticking.

# STIR-FRIED CHICKEN *with Cashews*

If you like Chinese food, you'll love this tasty combination of tender chicken, crunchy nuts, and crisp vegetables.

## INGREDIENTS

- 3 tbsp oil
- ¾ cup unsalted cashews
- 4 boneless, skinless chicken breasts, cut into ¾-inch cubes
- 1 red onion, peeled and sliced
- 1 carrot, peeled and cut into thin sticks
- 1 green pepper, deseeded and chopped
- 2 tsp sweet chili sauce
- 2 tbsp light soy sauce
- 1 tsp corn starch
- ¾ cup chicken stock

1 Heat 1 tablespoon of the oil in the wok and stir-fry the cashews for about 30 seconds until lightly browned. Remove the cashews with a metal spatula or slotted spoon and set aside on a plate.

2 Add another tablespoon of the oil to the wok and stir-fry the chicken over high heat for 5 minutes or until golden. Remove to the plate.

## CHECK YOUR SKILLS
- p. 6–7 for using knives
- p. 12 for using peelers
- p. 30 for stir-frying

3 Add the remaining tablespoon of oil and stir-fry the onion and carrot for 3 minutes. Add the green pepper and stir-fry for an additional 3 minutes.

4 Return the cashews and chicken to the wok and add the chili sauce.

5 In a small bowl, whisk the soy sauce with the corn starch until smooth and then add the stock.

**QUICK TIP...**Make sure the oil is nice and hot before you add your ingredients to the wok.

### TRY THIS!
Instead of chicken, you could use cubed lean pork or large raw peeled shrimp. If using shrimp, only stir-fry them for 2–3 minutes until they turn pinkish-white, as they cook more quickly.

6 Pour into the wok and toss everything together over the heat for 2–3 minutes until the sauce is bubbling. Serve at once.

SERVES 4

# BEEF TACOS

Tex-Mex food is tasty and fun to eat, so dishes like these beef tacos make the perfect finger food at a party.

## INGREDIENTS

**FOR THE BEEF FILLING:**
- 1 tbsp sunflower or canola oil
- 1 lb ground lean beef
- 1 green pepper, deseeded and chopped
- 1 quantity of rich tomato sauce (see recipe on page 8, leaving out the Parmesan cheese)

**TO SERVE:**
- 12 taco shells
- 1 quantity of guacamole (see recipe on page 26)
- 3 tomatoes, diced
- 1 small head of lettuce, shredded
- Grated cheddar cheese

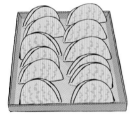

### YOU WILL NEED

Baking sheet
Large spoon
Spatula
Sauté pan
3 small serving bowls

1 To make the beef filling, heat the oil in a sauté pan, add the ground beef, and fry until browned.

2 Add the green pepper, fry for 5 minutes, and then add the tomato sauce. Simmer uncovered for 15 minutes, stirring occasionally.

### CHECK YOUR SKILLS

- p. 7 for slicing an onion
- p. 6 for cutting a tomato
- p. 13 for grating cheese
- p. 31 for sautéing

3 When ready to serve, preheat the oven to 350°F. Spread out the taco shells on a baking sheet and warm in the oven for 3–4 minutes.

4 Spoon the guacamole, shredded lettuce, diced tomatoes, and grated cheese into separate serving bowls.

**QUICK TIP...** Stir the ground beef occasionally as it browns, breaking up any lumps with your spatula.

**SERVES 4**

5 Spoon the ground beef into the taco shells, along with the guacamole, lettuce, chopped tomatoes, and grated cheese.

**TRY THIS!**
Instead of ground beef, make the filling with ground turkey or lamb.

# FRENCH TOAST

For a real treat, make French toast for breakfast. You can drizzle it with maple syrup and serve it with pieces of crisp-fried bacon, or sprinkle the cooked toast with a little powdered sugar and serve it with fresh fruit. Yum!

## INGREDIENTS

- 4 slices of white bread
- 1 egg
- ½ tsp ground cinnamon
- ¼ cup milk
- small pat of butter

1 Cut the slices of bread in half diagonally to make 8 triangles in total.

2 In a shallow dish, beat together the egg, milk, and cinnamon with a fork until evenly mixed.

## CHECK YOUR SKILLS

- p. 6–7 for using knives
- p. 30 for frying

**QUICK TIP...**Make sure the triangles of bread are completely coated in the egg mixture so that they are beautifully golden when fried.

3 Heat the butter in a frying pan or cast iron griddle.

4 When the butter has melted, dip each triangle of bread in the egg mixture until coated on each side.

5 Add the eggy bread to the pan and fry for 1 minute on each side until golden brown. Serve at once.

6 You can also add some fruit to your French toast. Try using raspberries, blueberries, strawberries, or banana slices.

**TRY THIS!**
Instead of cinnamon, add 1 teaspoon vanilla extract to the egg and milk.

**SERVES 4**

# HASH BROWNS

Hash browns are great served for brunch with scrambled eggs, bacon, tomatoes and ketchup!

## INGREDIENTS

- 4 medium potatoes, peeled
- 1 onion, peeled and finely chopped
- 1 egg, beaten
- Salt and pepper
- 3 tbsp canola, sunflower, or vegetable oil

### YOU WILL NEED

Clean tea towel
Large plate lined with paper towels
Fish spatula
Grater
Palette knife
Mixing bowl
Frying pan
Tablespoon

1 Lay a clean dish towel on the work surface and grate the potatoes onto this.

2 Twist the towel around the potatoes and squeeze it over the sink to remove excess liquid.

### CHECK YOUR SKILLS

- p. 7 for chopping onions
- p. 13 for using a grater
- p. 30 for frying

3 Put the potatoes in a mixing bowl and stir in the chopped onion and beaten egg, mixing well so that the potatoes and onion are coated with the egg. Season with a little salt and some pepper.

4 Heat the oil in a large frying pan and add tablespoons of the potato mixture, flattening down each mound with the back of the spoon to make a patty about a ½-inch thick.

**QUICK TIP...** When grating the potatoes, make sure not to let your fingers get too close to the teeth of the grater. When only about a quarter of a potato is left, push this onto a fork before continuing to grate.

**TRY THIS!**
Add some finely chopped red pepper and sliced green onions, or a finely chopped red onion, to the grated potatoes for extra flavor and color.

5 Fry for about 3 minutes until the patties have browned underneath, then turn them over with a palette knife and fry for an additional 3 minutes to brown the other side.

6 Lift the hash browns out of the pan with a fish spatula and drain on a plate lined with paper towels. Serve hot.

**SERVES 4**

# BOILING, STEAMING & POACHING

Boiling, steaming, and poaching are all done on the stove and, just like when frying, it's important to use the right size and shape of pan.

## TYPES OF PANS

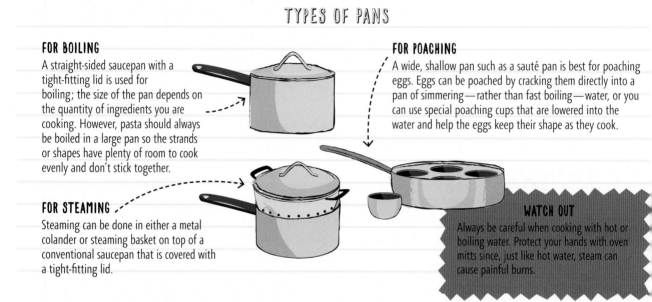

### FOR BOILING

A straight-sided saucepan with a tight-fitting lid is used for boiling; the size of the pan depends on the quantity of ingredients you are cooking. However, pasta should always be boiled in a large pan so the strands or shapes have plenty of room to cook evenly and don't stick together.

### FOR STEAMING

Steaming can be done in either a metal colander or steaming basket on top of a conventional saucepan that is covered with a tight-fitting lid.

### FOR POACHING

A wide, shallow pan such as a sauté pan is best for poaching eggs. Eggs can be poached by cracking them directly into a pan of simmering—rather than fast boiling—water, or you can use special poaching cups that are lowered into the water and help the eggs keep their shape as they cook.

### WATCH OUT

Always be careful when cooking with hot or boiling water. Protect your hands with oven mitts since, just like hot water, steam can cause painful burns.

## Technique 1: BOILING PASTA

Different types of pasta, such as spaghetti, penne, and bow tie, require different cooking times, so always check the instructions on the packet. Most dried pastas take around 10 minutes to cook, while fresh pastas only need a couple of minutes. Allow 3½–4 ounces of dried pasta or 5–6 ounces of fresh pasta per person.

*give it a stir!*

1 Fill a large saucepan about ²/₃ full with cold water. Place it on the stove and bring the water to a fast boil. Add half a teaspoon of salt.

2 Carefully add the pasta to the water. If it is a short-cut pasta such as penne, you can do this using a large spoon. If it's a long pasta, hold the bundle of pasta upright at one end and lower the other end into the water. Bend the pasta round as the part that is in the water starts to soften, pushing the remaining pasta gently into the water.

3 Boil for the length of time recommended on the packet, stirring occasionally to make sure the pasta is not sticking to the bottom of the pan.

4 To see if the pasta is ready, carefully lift out one piece with a fork and let it cool for a few moments before biting into it. The pasta should be tender but not too soft and still have a little bite —what Italians call "al dente."

5 Put a large colander in the sink and drain the pasta into this.

# Technique 2: STEAMING VEGETABLES

Vegetables such as broccoli, cauliflower, new potatoes, baby carrots, and peas are best steamed rather than boiled, since the steam cooks the vegetables just as quickly as boiling but none of the flavor is lost in the water. Be careful when you lift the lid of the steamer to check if the vegetables are cooked—hot steam will escape and could burn you.

**TAKE CARE!**

1 Prepare vegetables as necessary by peeling off their skins, trimming tough stalks, or removing peas or broad beans from their pods.

2 Slice or chop the vegetables into bite-sized pieces, dividing cauliflower and broccoli into small florets.

3 Half-fill a saucepan with cold water, place on the stove, and bring the water to the boil.

4 Put your vegetables into a steaming basket or colander and place this on top of the saucepan. Cover with a tight-fitting lid.

5 Cook for 5–10 minutes or until the vegetables are just tender. Pierce with a toothpick or the point of a knife to check if they're ready.

# Technique 3: POACHING EGGS

Poached eggs are delicious served on hot, buttered English muffins. You need to use a large pan: either a sauté pan or large saucepan. The fresher the eggs, the less they will spread when they're put into the water.

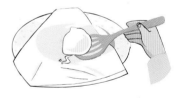

1 Half-fill a large pan with cold water, add 2 tablespoons of vinegar, and heat on the stove until the water comes to a simmer—small bubbles will appear over the surface.

2 While the water is heating, crack a fresh egg into a cup.

3 When the water reaches the right temperature, swirl it with a large spoon and slide the egg out of the cup and into the water. The swirling water will make the egg white curl and wrap itself around the yolk.

4 Leave to cook for 3–4 minutes, depending on how set you want the egg yolk to be. Carefully lift the egg from the water using a slotted spoon or a fish spatula and drain on a plate lined with paper towels.

## USING A POACHING CUP

1 Eggs can also be poached in special poaching cups. Lightly grease the cups with oil and crack an egg into each.

2 Float the cups in a shallow pan of simmering water. Cover the pan with a lid and leave until the eggs are cooked.

3 Protecting your hand with an oven mitt, lift out the cups with a fish spatula before scooping out the poached eggs.

mmm...tasty!

# EGGS BENEDICT

Ham and poached eggs on toasted English muffins topped with creamy hollandaise sauce is a brunch that the entire family will love. Make it for your mom for extra brownie points!

## YOU WILL NEED
*Bread knife*

*Large plate lined with kitchen paper*

*Large spoon*

*Large saucepan or sauté pan*

*Small bowl*

*Slotted spoon or fish spatula*

*Butter knife*

## INGREDIENTS
- 4 large eggs
- 2 English muffins
- 8 tbsp hollandaise sauce
- 3 tbsp butter
- 8 thin slices of ham

1 Follow the technique for poaching an egg in a poaching cup (see page 37) cooking all four eggs together in the pan over a gentle heat for 3-4 minutes.

2 While the eggs are cooking, cut the muffins in half and toast them. Microwave the hollandaise sauce in a small bowl on low power for about 1 minute until warm, but not bubbling.

## CHECK YOUR SKILLS
- p. 42 for grilling
- p. 37 for poaching eggs

3 Spread butter on the cut sides of the muffins and put them on serving plates. Arrange the ham slices on top.

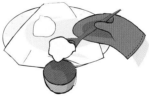

4 Lift the eggs from the pan and drain briefly on a plate lined with paper towels.

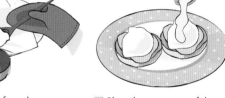

5 Place the egg on top of the ham and spoon the hollandaise sauce over the egg. Serve at once.

**QUICK TIP...** Jars of readymade hollandaise sauce are easy to find in supermarkets.

**TRY THIS!**
For a vegetarian version of eggs benedict, replace the slices of ham with cooked spinach. Rinse and chop fresh spinach leaves (about ¼ cup per person), put them in a microwaveable bowl, and cook for 2 minutes until the leaves have wilted.

**SERVES 4**

*Breakfast is served!*

# PERFECT PASTA with
# Creamy Mushroom Sauce

You can serve this mushroom sauce with any type of pasta—spaghetti, linguine, tagliatelle, or short pasta such as shells or bows.

## INGREDIENTS

- 2 tbsp olive oil or sunflower oil
- 1 red onion, peeled and thinly sliced
- $\frac{1}{2}$ cup button mushrooms, quartered
- $1\frac{1}{3}$ cup chicken stock, made from a stock cube
- 1 lb dried penne pasta
- 1 tsp corn starch
- 4 tbsp sour cream or Greek yogurt

TO SERVE:
- Grated Parmesan cheese

## YOU WILL NEED

Cook's knife
Chopping board
Colander
Large saucepan
Sauté pan
Small bowl
Spoon

1 Heat the oil in a sauté pan, add the onion, and cover the pan. Cook for 5 minutes or until the onion has started to soften. Take the lid off the pan, add the mushrooms, and cook for another 5 minutes, stirring occasionally.

2 Add the stock and leave to simmer over low heat with the lid on the pan. While this is simmering, cook the spaghetti, following the instructions on the packet.

## CHECK YOUR SKILLS

- p. 7 for slicing onions
- p. 13 for grating cheese
- p. 31 for sautéing
- p. 36 for boiling pasta

SERVES 4

**QUICK TIP...**Before you quarter the mushrooms, put them in a colander and run cold water over them to rinse them. Pat the mushrooms dry with paper towels.

3 In a small bowl, stir the corn starch into the sour cream or yogurt and add to the pan. Stir until evenly blended in, bring back to a simmer, and cook for another 2 minutes.

4 Drain the cooked pasta and stir it into the mushroom sauce until all the noodles are coated. Spoon into serving dishes and serve at once, sprinkled with grated Parmesan cheese.

**TRY THIS!**
Instead of pasta, serve the delicious sauce spooned over roasted chicken legs.

# STEAMED ASIAN DUMPLINGS

## YOU WILL NEED

Steamer

Cook's knife

Chopping board

Teaspoon

Pastry brush

Mixing bowl

## CHECK YOUR SKILLS

- p. 7 for chopping
- p. 37 for steaming

Time to practice your chopstick skills! For a full dinner, serve these little dumplings with the Vegetable Fried Rice on page 41.

## INGREDIENTS

- 6 oz ground chicken or pork
- ¼ cup cooked shrimp, finely chopped
- 2 green onions, finely chopped
- 2 tsp fresh ginger, peeled and very finely chopped (or 1 tsp store-bought ginger purée)
- 2 tbsp soy sauce
- 5 water chestnuts, from a can, drained and finely chopped
- 30 wonton wrappers
- 1 egg white, lightly whisked

TO SERVE:
- Soy sauce, for dipping

1 Put the ground chicken or pork in a bowl and stir in the chopped shrimp, green onions, ginger, soy sauce, and chopped water chestnuts.

2 Lay a wonton wrapper on a chopping board and spoon 1 teaspoon of the mixture in the center.

**QUICK TIP...** If you find you have some filling left, make a few more wontons rather than adding extra filling to the ones already completed. If the wrappers are over-filled, they could burst or split when steamed.

3 Brush the edges of the wrapper with egg white and gather them up around the filling to enclose it. Pinch the edges of the wrapper together at the top to seal it. Repeat with the remaining wrappers and filling.

4 Arrange the dumplings in a Chinese (or other) steamer without them touching—you may need to cook them in batches —and steam for 5 minutes.

5 Serve the dumplings hot with a bowl of extra soy sauce for dipping.

**MAKES ABOUT 30**

**TRY THIS!** You can vary the filling in the dumplings by adding different ingredients. Try chopped mushrooms or red pepper instead of shrimp, and a chopped shallot instead of green onions. If you like garlic, you can stir in a couple of crushed cloves. Just remember to chop everything as finely as you can.

# VEGETABLE FRIED RICE

Fried rice is a great Chinese takeout favorite and you can switch it up by adding different vegetables, prawns, pork, or chicken. Whatever you add, make sure to chop all the ingredients into small, similar-sized pieces so they cook evenly.

## INGREDIENTS

- 1¾ cup long grain rice
- ½ tsp salt
- 2 tbsp canola or sunflower oil
- ½ red pepper, deseeded and finely chopped
- ½ green pepper, deseeded and finely chopped
- ½ cup button mushrooms, thinly sliced
- 1 cup sweet corn kernels
- 1 cup frozen peas
- 4 green onions, finely chopped
- 2 large eggs, beaten
- 2 tbsp oyster sauce or light soy sauce

**YOU WILL NEED**

Sieve

Saucepan with a lid

Wok or large frying pan

Metal spatula or large spoon

Fork

**1** Put the rice into a sieve and run cold water over it until the water is clear.

**2** Pour the rice into a saucepan and add 3 cups cold water and ½ teaspoon salt. Stir once, then bring to a boil. Turn the heat down as low as it will go and cover the pan with a lid. Cook the rice for 10–15 minutes without taking the lid off the pan, until the rice is tender and has absorbed the water.

### CHECK YOUR SKILLS

- p. 6 for using knives
- p. 36 for boiling
- p. 30 for stir-frying

**QUICK TIP...** It's not necessary to thaw the frozen peas before you add them. They'll soon defrost when mixed with the other hot vegetables.

**3** Heat the oil in a wok or large frying pan and, using a metal spatula or large spoon, stir-fry the red and green peppers over a fairly high heat for 3 minutes. Add the mushrooms and stir-fry for 2 minutes.

**4** Add the sweet corn, frozen peas, and green onions and stir-fry for 2 minutes. Push the vegetables to one side of the pan and pour in the eggs. Leave until they start to set, then scramble them by stirring with a fork.

**5** Mix the egg with the vegetables and add the rice and oyster or soy sauce. Toss everything together over the direct heat for 2 minutes, spoon into serving bowls, and serve at once.

SERVES 2-4

# GRILLING, ROASTING & BAKING

Grilling is a quick way of cooking small cuts of meat or fish, while roasting involves longer cooking time for larger cuts of meat or vegetables in the oven. Baking is cooking bread, cakes, pastry, and cookies in the oven—in fact, everything that you'd buy at a bakery!

## EQUIPMENT NEEDED

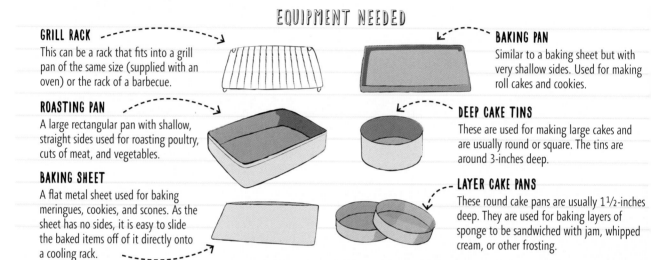

**GRILL RACK**
This can be a rack that fits into a grill pan of the same size (supplied with an oven) or the rack of a barbecue.

**ROASTING PAN**
A large rectangular pan with shallow, straight sides used for roasting poultry, cuts of meat, and vegetables.

**BAKING SHEET**
A flat metal sheet used for baking meringues, cookies, and scones. As the sheet has no sides, it is easy to slide the baked items off of it directly onto a cooling rack.

**BAKING PAN**
Similar to a baking sheet but with very shallow sides. Used for making roll cakes and cookies.

**DEEP CAKE TINS**
These are used for making large cakes and are usually round or square. The tins are around 3-inches deep.

**LAYER CAKE PANS**
These round cake pans are usually 1½-inches deep. They are used for baking layers of sponge to be sandwiched with jam, whipped cream, or other frosting.

## Technique 1: SETTING UP THE GRILL TRAY

Grilling is done by placing food on an open wire rack with a high heat coming either from above, if using a conventional kitchen grill, or below, if using a barbecue.

1 For a kitchen grill, fit the rack into its tray and attach the handle to the tray if one is provided. You can line the grill rack with foil if you want to spoon any juices that run out over the food as it cooks.

*Optional: line the grill with foil to catch the juices.*

2 Heat up the grill. If you're using a gas grill, you can adjust the flames according to the level of heat you need. If you're using an electric grill, you'll need to position the tray close to the heat if you want the food to cook very quickly, but lower it if, once browned, the food needs to cook more slowly.

3 Place your steaks, burgers, kebabs, or whatever you are cooking on the grill rack in a single layer, without the items touching.

4 Grill one side of the food until it is browned, but watch it carefully to make sure it doesn't burn. Then turn it over with tongs to cook the other side.

## Technique 2: USING BAKING PARCHMENT

Baking parchment is a special kitchen paper that has a silicone coating to prevent baked items such as cookies, cakes, and meringues from sticking to baking sheets or cake pans. Both sides of the parchment are non-stick, which means there is no right or wrong side.

1 To line a baking sheet, brush the sheet lightly with a flavorless oil, such as sunflower or vegetable. Cut a piece of baking parchment slightly smaller than the size of the sheet and lay this on top, smoothing it out evenly. The oil stops the parchment from sliding around.

2 To line a deep, round cake pan, place the pan on a sheet of baking parchment and draw around the base. Using kitchen scissors, cut around just inside the drawn line.

3 Measure the circumference of the pan by wrapping a length of string around the sides and cutting it so that it is 1 inch longer. Cut a strip of parchment the same length as the string and 2 inches deeper than the pan.

4 Fold over the strip, 1 inch from the bottom. Open the fold and make cuts, about 1 inch apart, with scissors, as deep as the crease you have just made.

5 Brush the inside of the pan lightly with oil. Take the long strip of parchment and angle it into the pan with the cuts at the bottom. Make sure it sticks smoothly around the sides with no creases and the cuts lie flat around the bottom of the pan.

6 Slide the round piece of parchment into the pan to cover the base, laying it over the cut sections at the bottom.

## Technique 3: ROASTING A CHICKEN IN FOIL

Covering a chicken with foil for the first part of the roasting time ensures the flesh cooks evenly and doesn't dry out.

*BE CAREFUL WHEN REMOVING THE FOIL FROM THE CHICKEN AS HOT STEAM CAN GIVE NASTY BURNS.*

*Wash your hands after handling raw chicken*

1 Weigh the chicken to calculate the total roasting time, allowing 25 minutes per 1 lb plus an additional 25 minutes.

2 Stand the chicken in a roasting pan and cover it loosely with a sheet of foil. Tuck the foil under the rim of the roasting pan to secure it in place, and make sure the foil forms a "tent" over the chicken and isn't sticking to the skin.

3 Preheat the oven to 400°F and roast the chicken for the calculated time, carefully removing the foil for the final 25 minutes so the skin becomes brown and crisp.

4 To check the chicken is fully cooked, push a skewer into the thickest part of one of the legs—the juices that run out should be clear and not pink. Turn off the oven and leave the chicken inside for 10 minutes to rest before serving.

*DON'T FORGET TO WEAR OVEN MITTS WHEN TAKING ANYTHING OUT OF A HOT OVEN.*

# MINI PITA PIZZAS

## YOU WILL NEED

Cook's knife

Chopping board

Spoon or round-bladed knife to spread the tomato sauce

Pastry brush

Grater, if grating the mozzarella

These mini pizzas are the perfect after-school snack—quick and easy to make and fun to eat. You can try out the toppings in this recipe, or add any others you like.

## INGREDIENTS

- 8 mini pitas
- 4 tbsp tomato sauce
- 2 tomatoes, sliced
- ½ green pepper, deseeded and cut into thin slices
- 4 button mushrooms, sliced
- 2 tbsp extra virgin olive oil
- 2 tsp dried oregano or mixed herbs
- 1 cup mozzarella cheese, grated or sliced

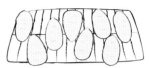

1 Arrange the pitas on the grill rack in a single layer.

2 Spread the tomato sauce, leaving a ½ inch from the edge of the pitas bare.

## CHECK YOUR SKILLS

- p. 6 for slicing tomatoes
- p. 13 for using graters
- p. 42 for grilling

3 Top with the mushroom, green pepper, and tomato slices, dividing them evenly.

4 Brush the vegetables with the olive oil and sprinkle the herbs over the pitas.

5 Top with the grated or sliced mozzarella and grill until the cheese melts. Serve at once.

*Finger food!*

SERVES 4

### TRY THIS!

Pepperoni, chopped ham, corn kernels, red onion slices, and salami all make great pizza toppings. You can use grated cheddar cheese instead of mozzarella if you prefer.

**QUICK TIP...** You can make as many or as few pita pizzas as you like. All you need to do is use less or more of the topping ingredients. You'll quickly get the hang of how much you need to make one or two pizzas.

# CHICKEN SATAY

These spicy chicken kebabs are grilled on open-air barbecues in Thailand and Malaysia, where they are enjoyed as quick and tasty street food. You can cook them in your kitchen grill or outdoors on a barbecue when the weather is nice.

## INGREDIENTS

FOR THE CHICKEN SATAY:
- 4 boneless chicken breasts, skinned
- 1-inch piece of root ginger, peeled and grated or finely chopped
- 2 cloves of garlic, peeled and crushed
- 2 tbsp brown sugar
- Juice of 1 lime
- 2 tbsp soy sauce
- 2 tsp canola or vegetable oil, plus extra for brushing

FOR THE PEANUT SAUCE:
- 1 small onion, peeled and finely chopped
- 1 tbsp canola or vegetable oil
- 1 tsp chili sauce
- 2 tbsp soy sauce
- 2/3 cup peanut butter, smooth or crunchy
- Juice of 1 lime
- 2/3 cup water

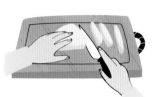

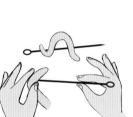

**1** To make the chicken satay, cut the chicken into thin strips across the breasts and place in a bowl or shallow dish.

**2** Mix together the ginger, garlic, brown sugar, lime juice, soy sauce, and oil in a small bowl and pour over the chicken. Cover the bowl with cling wrap and leave the chicken to marinate for 1 hour or longer.

**3** Lift out the chicken and thread the pieces onto the skewers to make "S" shapes. Brush with oil and lay side by side on the grill rack. Grill for 5 minutes, using tongs to turn the skewers over once or twice.

**4** To make the sauce, fry the onion in the oil in a small saucepan until it is soft and golden brown. Add the rest of the ingredients and stir constantly over a low heat for 2 minutes until hot and the sauce is evenly mixed. Serve the chicken kebabs with the warm sauce.

**YOU WILL NEED**

Cook's knife
Chopping board
Cling wrap
12 metal or wooden skewers
Tongs
Pastry brush
Small bowl
Large spoon
Small saucepan
Large bowl

**CHECK YOUR SKILLS**
- p. 7 for chopping onions
- p. 19 for juicing
- p. 31 for frying onions
- p. 42 for using the grill

SERVES 4-6

**QUICK TIP...** You can use either metal or wooden skewers, but soak wooden skewers in water for 30 minutes first (so they don't burn) or cover the ends with foil.

# CHOCOLATE CHIP COOKIES

Soft and chewy in the middle, crisp on the outside, and studded with chocolate chips—it's not surprising these cookies are everyone's favorite. They won't hang around in the cookie jar for long!

## YOU WILL NEED

- 2 baking sheets
- Wire cooling rack
- Wooden spoon or electric mixer
- Large metal spoon
- Palette knife
- Mixing bowl
- Sieve
- Baking parchment

## INGREDIENTS

- A little canola or sunflower oil, for greasing
- 1¼ stick butter, cut into small pieces and softened
- ½ cup light soft brown sugar
- ½ cup caster sugar
- 1 large egg
- 1 tsp vanilla extract
- 1¼ cups dark chocolate chips
- 1⅔ cups self-rising flour

1 Preheat the oven to 375°F. Brush two baking sheets lightly with oil and line with baking parchment.

2 Beat the butter and sugars together in a mixing bowl until light and fluffy. Beat in the egg and vanilla extract and then stir in the chocolate chips.

**CHECK YOUR SKILLS**
- p. 52 for beating butter and sugar together
- p. 43 for baking

3 Sift in the flour and stir it in with a large metal spoon until all the ingredients are evenly mixed.

4 Place 12 small mounds of the batter onto each baking sheet, leaving plenty of space between each one since the cookies will spread when they bake. Make each into a round shape and flatten slightly on top with the back of the spoon.

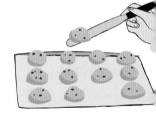

5 Bake for about 10 minutes or until the cookies are golden. Allow to cool on the baking sheets for 5 minutes before lifting them off with a palette knife and transferring to a wire rack to cool completely.

**MAKES 24 COOKIES**

**QUICK TIP...** The cookies are ready to come out of the oven when browning at the edges but still a little soft in the center.

**TRY THIS!** For some really indulgent cookies, use a mixture of white, milk, and dark chocolate chips.

# ROASTED MEDITERRANEAN
## Vegetables

Not a fan of boring, boiled veggies that taste like they've been cooked for a month? This colorful mix of roasted vegetables will be a party for your taste buds! It's great as a side dish for pork chops or chicken legs.

## YOU WILL NEED

Measuring spoons

Cook's knife

Mixing bowl

Chopping board

Large spoon

Roasting pan

## INGREDIENTS

- 4 tbsp olive oil
- 1 red onion, peeled and cut into wedges
- 1 each red, orange, and yellow peppers, halved, seeds removed, and cut into 1-inch pieces
- ½ cup mushrooms, halved or quartered
- 2 medium zucchinis, ends trimmed off and thickly sliced
- 1 small eggplant, stalk removed and cut into 1-inch pieces
- 1 tbsp balsamic or white wine vinegar

1 Measure 3 tablespoons of the olive oil into a large bowl and add the onion wedges, peppers, mushrooms, zucchinis, and eggplant chunks. Stir well until the vegetables are coated in the oil.

2 Preheat the oven to 400°F. Spoon the vegetables into a roasting pan and spread them out in an even layer.

## CHECK YOUR SKILLS

- p. 6–7 for preparing vegetables
- p. 42–43 for roasting

3 Roast the vegetables in the oven for 35–40 minutes or until they are tender and brown at the edges.

4 Mix together the remaining tablespoon of olive oil with the vinegar. Take the vegetables out of the oven and drizzle the dressing over them.

### TRY THIS!

Halloumi is a semi-hard cheese from Cyprus that can be heated to a high temperature without melting. Cut a halloumi cheese into ¼-inch slices and cook the slices in a hot griddle pan for 1–2 minutes on each side until scorched with brown lines. Serve the hot cheese slices with the vegetables.

**SERVES 4–6**

5 Spoon the vegetables into a serving dish and serve hot, or leave to cool before serving.

Lip-smackingly good

# SKILL 8

# MAKING SWEET & SAVORY SAUCES

Nobody wants a lumpy sauce to spoil their cooking. From making a smooth and creamy sauce to add to a savory dish to jazzing up a dessert with a homemade fruit purée, there will be no stopping you once you have the knack for it.

## EQUIPMENT NEEDED

### MILK PAN
This saucepan has one or two pouring lips to prevent milk or other hot liquids from spilling when you pour them out of the pan.

### MEASURING CUP
You'll need this to measure the exact quantity of liquid you need to make a sauce.

### WIRE SIEVE
A fine mesh sieve with a handle is used to seive the pips and seeds out of a fruit purée.

### HEATPROOF BOWL AND SAUCEPAN
Chocolate will spoil if it gets too hot, so it's best to melt it in a heatproof bowl on top of a saucepan.

### FLAT WHISK
This type of whisk can reach into the corners of a saucepan to stop lumps of flour collecting there and making your sauce lumpy.

## Technique 1: MAKING CHOCOLATE SAUCE

You can drizzle chocolate sauce over all sorts of desserts to make them more special—vanilla ice cream, plain sponge cake, brownies, cheesecakes, or fresh fruit—you name it! The sauce can be served warm or cold.

Make sure you use a heat-proof bowl.

1 Chop 11 oz of dark chocolate or break it into small pieces.

2 Place the chocolate in a heatproof bowl and add ¾ cup of heavy cream, 2 tablespoons of syrup, and 1 tablespoon of butter.

3 Put a saucepan, one-third filled with water, on the stove and bring the water to a gentle simmer.

4 Stand the bowl on top of the saucepan, making sure the bottom of the bowl does not touch the water. Leave it there until the chocolate, syrup, and butter have melted, stirring occasionally until you have a smooth sauce.

5 Serve the chocolate sauce right away while it is still warm, or leave it to cool, stirring occasionally.

### EASY DOES IT
If chocolate gets too hot as it melts, it will develop an unattractive, grainy texture, so make sure the bottom of the bowl is above the water and do not let the water in the saucepan bubble hard. It should only be simmering gently.

The bowl should form a tight seal with the top of the pan. This is so that no steam can escape from the pan and cause moisture to come into contact with the melting mixture in the bowl.

# Technique 2: MAKING A WHITE SAUCE

A plain white sauce can be flavored with different ingredients, such as grated cheese, chopped parsley, or sliced mushrooms. Cheese sauce is the most popular white sauce, since it can be used in many different dishes. It's particularly tasty in baked pasta dishes such as lasagna, cannelloni, or macaroni and cheese (page 51).

1 To make a white sauce to serve 4 people, melt 2 tablespoons of butter in a saucepan on the stove over a low heat. When the butter has melted, take the saucepan off the heat and stir in 3½ tablespoons of plain flour or corn starch to make a smooth mixture—this is called a "roux."

2 Put the saucepan back on a low heat and cook the roux gently for 2 minutes so that it bubbles gently but does not change color.

3 Remove the pan from the heat again and gradually stir in 1 cup of milk. Keep stirring until the mixture is smooth and there are no lumps.

4 Put the pan back on the stove and turn up the heat to medium. Bring the sauce to a boil, stirring continuously, until it is thick, glossy, and smooth. Cook for another minute.

5 Season the sauce with a little salt and some freshly ground white pepper. Stir in grated cheese or other flavorings off the heat.

**WATCH OUT FOR LUMPS!**
Use a wooden spoon or—even better—a flat sauce whisk to get into the corners of the pan. You must stir the sauce constantly as it comes to a boil. If any lumps form, take the pan off the heat and beat the sauce as vigorously as you can. Once the sauce has boiled, the only way to get rid of lumps is to use a handheld mixer.

# Technique 3: MAKING A FRUIT PURÉE

A purée, also known as a "coulis," is a sweet, smooth fruit sauce made by simmering fresh or dried fruit in water or another liquid, such as fruit juice, until the fruit is soft. The fruit and liquid is then blended together to make a smooth purée, using a food processor or handheld mixer. If necessary, it is then sifted to remove any skin or seeds. Fruit that is already soft, such as raspberries or strawberries, doesn't need to be cooked first. It can simply be puréed, sifted, and then thinned to the right consistency with cold water or fruit juice.

1 To make a strawberry purée to serve 4 people, remove the hulls from 1 cup of ripe strawberries.

2 Put the strawberries in a standing blender (or use a bowl and handheld mixer), add ½ cup of apple or orange juice, or cold water, and 3½ tablespoons of powdered sugar.

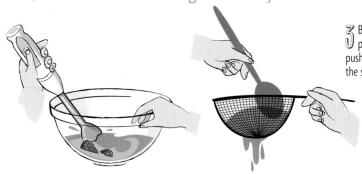

3 Blend until you have a smooth purée and serve it as it is or push it through a sieve to remove the seeds.

4 Taste the purée after you've made it and adjust the sweetness by stirring in a little extra powdered sugar or a spoonful of honey, if needed.

# APRICOT PURÉE with Yogurt & Toasted Oats

## YOU WILL NEED

Saucepan with a lid

Handheld mixer, standing blender, or food processor

Spoon

Frying pan

6 tumblers

This recipe is fun if you want something a little different for breakfast, and it also makes a great dessert. Make them in tumblers or other glasses so you can see all the colorful layers.

## INGREDIENTS

- 1¼ cup ready-to-eat dried apricots
- 1 cup fresh orange juice
- 2 tbsp butter
- 2 oz quick-cook oats
- 1½ oz chopped hazelnuts
- 2 tbsp light soft brown sugar
- 2 tbsp honey
- 1 cup thick Greek yogurt

1 Put the apricots in a saucepan and pour over the orange juice. Put a lid on the pan and simmer the apricots for 15 minutes until they are soft.

2 Leave the apricots to cool and then blend the contents of the pan to make a smooth purée.

## CHECK YOUR SKILLS

- p. 49 for making a fruit purée

**SERVES 6**

3 Melt the butter in a frying pan, add the oats and hazelnuts, and spread them out with the back of the spoon. Cook for 1–2 minutes until the oats and nuts are lightly toasted, stirring frequently.

4 Sprinkle the brown sugar into the pan of oats and nuts and cook for an additional 1 minute. Remove from the heat and leave to cool.

5 Stir the honey into the yogurt until evenly mixed in.

*Yum yum!*

**QUICK TIP...**Instead of using only apricots, you could make the purée with 6 oz apricots and 1 apple, peeled, cored, and chopped, cooking and then blending the two fruits together with the orange juice.

6 Layer up the apricot purée with the yogurt and the oat mixture in six tumblers, finishing with a sprinkling of the oat mixture on the top of each one. Chill until ready to serve.

# MACARONI & CHEESE with Cherry Tomatoes

Mac 'n' Cheese will always be a family favorite as long as the cook uses plenty of rich cheese to coat the macaroni. Including cherry tomatoes in the mix doesn't just add extra flavor; the vibrant red tomatoes make it look good too.

## YOU WILL NEED

*Large spoon*  *Grater*

*Large saucepan*  *Measuring jug*

*Large ovenproof dish*

## INGREDIENTS

- ½ lb macaroni
- 2 tbsp butter
- 2 tbsp plain flour
- 2½ cup milk
- 2 cups strong mature Cheddar cheese, grated
- ⅓ cup cherry tomatoes, halved
- 2 tbsp grated Parmesan cheese

1 Cook the macaroni in a large saucepan of boiling water according to the packet instructions. Drain and set aside.

2 Heat the butter in the saucepan over a low heat until it melts.

## CHECK YOUR SKILLS

- p. 12 for grating
- p. 36 for boiling pasta
- p. 49 for making a white sauce

3 Take the pan off the heat and stir in the flour until you have a smooth mixture. Cook this gently so it bubbles over a low heat for 2 minutes.

4 Remove the pan from the heat and gradually stir in the milk until the mixture is completely smooth. Put the pan back over a medium heat and bring to a boil, stirring all the time to prevent any lumps from forming in your sauce. Simmer for 1 minute.

5 Stir the macaroni, ⅔ cup of the cheddar cheese, and the halved tomatoes into the sauce and spoon the mixture into an ovenproof dish. Sprinkle the rest of the cheddar and the Parmesan over the top.

6 Preheat the oven to 400°F and bake for 30 minutes or until bubbling hot and golden and crispy on top. Serve at once.

**SERVES 4**

**QUICK TIP...** If you think your sauce is in danger of becoming lumpy, take the saucepan off the heat and stir or whisk until it is smooth again before continuing. If the sauce looks like it is about to bubble over, take the pan off the heat, and turn the heat down before putting the pan back on.

# BEATING, WHIPPING & WHISKING

Beating, whipping, and whisking are all slightly different, depending on what equipment and ingredients you use. They are important skills to master, as you'll use them for lots of recipes.

### BEATING

This usually applies to mixtures that contain whole eggs such as cake batters and puddings. You "beat" to mix ingredients together until everything is evenly combined. Beating is also used to make flavored butters.

### WHIPPING

Whipping is done with a whisk to add air to a mixture, changing its texture and increasing its volume. It usually applies to cream, which is whipped until thickened enough to hold its shape.

### WHISKING

Technically this is the same as whipping, but the difference is that cream is "whipped" but whole eggs or egg whites are "whisked" to make omelettes and meringues.

## EQUIPMENT NEEDED

**WOODEN SPOON**
Ideal for beating a mixture until smooth.

**BALLOON WHISK**
Easy to use and great for whipping air into a mixture.

**HANDHELD MIXER**
A quick way to mix ingredients. The blades are easy to remove for cleaning.

## Technique 1: BEATING BUTTER AND SUGAR TOGETHER

This technique is used when making sponge cake and buttercream frosting. It involves beating the measured butter and sugar together until they are pale in color and fluffy. Not only does it mix the butter and sugar evenly, it also beats in air so the baked cake or buttercream has a beautifully light texture.

1 Take the butter out of the fridge about 30 minutes before you need it. Measure the amount you need and return the rest to the fridge. Cut your butter into small pieces and leave to soften.

2 Put the butter in a mixing bowl and beat it with a wooden spoon or handheld mixer until it is smooth.

3 Add the sugar to the beaten butter.

4 Beat the sugar and butter together until they combine to make a light, fluffy mixture that is pale in color.

# Technique 2: WHIPPING CREAM

You can whip cream to add to desserts, cakes, and even to top a bowl of soup. Use heavy cream or whipping cream, but don't use half and half or light cream because they won't thicken up.

*stir the whisk in circles*

1 Pour your heavy or whipping cream into a mixing bowl.

2 Using a balloon whisk in a circular motion, whip the cream until it stands in soft peaks that hold their shape.

3 Alternatively, whip the cream using a handheld mixer set on medium speed. As soon as the cream starts to thicken, reduce the speed to low and continue until the cream holds its shape.

4 If you over-whip cream it will become grainy and start to separate. If this happens, stir in 1–2 tablespoons of cold milk until the cream stands in soft peaks again.

# Technique 3: WHISKING EGG WHITES

Egg whites must be whisked in a clean mixing bowl as any grease sticking to the sides of the bowl will prevent the whites from whisking. Make sure no yolk gets into the whites before you whisk them.

1 Take your eggs out of the fridge about 30 minutes before you need them so they have time to come to room temperature—this will make the whites easier to whisk.

2 Tap the egg on the side of a clean, dry bowl, and carefully pull the shell apart. Tip the egg onto a small plate or saucer.

3 Place one half of the shell over the yolk and tilt the plate so just the white slides off into the bowl. Repeat with the rest of the eggs.

4 Whisk the egg whites using a balloon whisk or handheld mixer on medium speed until the whites stand in soft or stiff peaks, depending on the recipe you are making.

# CHOCOLATE Sponge Cake

## YOU WILL NEED

Wire cooling rack

Sieve

Mixing bowl

Wooden spoon or handheld mixer

Pastry brush

Measuring spoons

Palette knife

Large spoon

Two 8-inch layer cake pans

Baking parchment

You could make this cake to celebrate a birthday and decorate it for the person you're giving it to. Don't forget the candles!

## INGREDIENTS

**FOR THE CAKE MIXTURE:**
- 1½ sticks butter, cut into small pieces and softened
- ¾ cup light, soft brown sugar
- 3 large eggs
- 1⅓ cups plain flour
- 1 ½ tbsp cocoa powder
- 1 ½ tsp baking powder

**TO FILL AND FROST THE CAKE:**
- 10½ tbsp butter, cut into small pieces and softened
- 2½ cups powdered sugar, sifted
- 2 oz dark chocolate, melted
- 1 tbsp cocoa powder
- 1 tbsp milk

1 Preheat the oven to 350°F. Line the bases of your cake pans with parchment.

2 Beat the butter in a mixing bowl until smooth and then beat in the brown sugar until light and fluffy.

5 Divide the mixture between the cake pans, spreading the top level, and bake for 25–30 minutes. Push a toothpick into the center of each cake layer. It's ready if it comes out clean.

6 Cool the cakes in the pans for 15 minutes before turning out onto a wire rack to cool completely. Peel off the lining paper.

3 Beat in the eggs one at a time, adding a tablespoon of flour with each egg to stop the mixture from curdling.

4 Sift in the rest of the flour with the cocoa powder and baking powder, and stir until mixed in.

7 To make the buttercream frosting, beat the butter until smooth. Gradually beat in the powdered sugar and, when it has all been added, beat in the melted chocolate, cocoa powder, and milk.

8 Sandwich the cake layers with the frosting and spread it evenly over the top and sides with a palette knife.

## CHECK YOUR SKILLS

- p. 52 for beating
- p. 48 for melting chocolate
- p. 42–43 for using the oven

*Rich!*

SERVES 8-10

**QUICK TIP...** As these tins are shallower than ordinary cake tins, you only need to line the bases with baking parchment. Some tins also have loose bottoms, which makes it much easier to turn out the cakes.

# MERINGUE with Strawberries & Cream

Meringue doesn't just taste delicious, it looks impressive too. Top it with strawberries or other fruits, such as raspberries or kiwi.

## INGREDIENTS

- 3 egg whites
- ¾ cup fine or powdered sugar
- 1 tsp vinegar
- 1 tsp corn starch
- Oil for brushing

FOR THE FILLING:
- 1 cup heavy cream, whipped
- 1 cup strawberries, halved if large

## YOU WILL NEED

Baking parchment
Baking sheet

Large mixing bowl

Balloon whisk or handheld mixer

Metal tablespoon

Fish spatula

1 Preheat the oven to 300°F. Using a plate as a guide, draw an 8-inch circle on a sheet of baking parchment. Turn the parchment over and place it on a lightly greased baking sheet.

2 Put the egg whites in a large mixing bowl that is clean and dry. Using a balloon whisk or handheld mixer on medium speed, whisk the egg whites until they stand in soft peaks.

## CHECK YOUR SKILLS

- p. 53 for whisking egg whites
- p. 53 for whipping cream
- p. 42–43 for using the oven

3 Begin adding the sugar 1 teaspoon at a time until the mixture starts to feel thicker, then whisk in the rest of the sugar in a slow, steady stream. Whisk in the vinegar and corn starch with the last of the sugar.

4 Spoon the meringue over the marked circle you have drawn on the baking parchment, making a slight dip in the center with the back of the spoon.

**QUICK TIP...** Brushing a little oil on the baking sheet helps to keep the parchment in place.

*yummy!*

SERVES 6

5 Bake the meringue for 1 hour or until it is crisp. Leave it to cool completely in the turned-off oven before carefully easing it off the parchment with a fish spatula and placing it on a serving plate. A traditional meringue is crisp on the outside but chewy in the center.

# CHEESE OMELETTE

## YOU WILL NEED

*Omelette pan (a small frying pan with sloping sides, preferably non-stick)*

*Palette knife*        Fork

*Bowl*                  *Grater*

Omelettes make very popular brunch or lunch dishes. They're quick and easy, and you can add all sorts of ingredients to them that will keep even the fussiest eaters happy.

## INGREDIENTS

• 2–3 eggs, depending on how hungry you are
• A little salt and freshly ground black pepper
• 1 tbsp butter
• 6 tbsp mature cheddar cheese, grated

1 Crack the eggs into a bowl, add a little salt and some freshly ground black pepper, and beat them with a fork until the yolks and whites are well mixed and the eggs are frothy.

2 Put the omelette pan on the stove over a medium heat. Add the butter and wait until it melts and foams.

## CHECK YOUR SKILLS

• p. 13 for grating cheese
• p. 30 for frying

3 Pour in the beaten eggs and cook for about 30 seconds or until the eggs are lightly set on the bottom but still liquid on top.

4 As the eggs start to set, push the outer edges to the center with a fork, so that the uncooked egg runs to the outside and cooks. Repeat this until the egg is cooked but still soft in the center.

5 Sprinkle the grated cheese onto the center of the omelette. Increase the heat to high and cook for another 30 seconds so the omelette browns underneath and the cheese melts.

## TRY THIS!

Here are some other delicious things you can add to an omelette:
• 1 slice of ham, chopped into small pieces
• 1 cup sliced mushrooms, sautéed in olive oil first, until softened
• 2 bacon strips or 1 large sausage, grilled and chopped into small pieces
• 1 tomato, diced, plus 2 fresh basil leaves, shredded.

6 Slide a palette knife around one side of the omelette and fold it over in half. Take the pan off the heat and tilt it slightly to one side so the folded omelette moves to the edge of the pan. Slide it out of the pan onto a plate and serve it right away.

**QUICK TIP...** After you've added the butter to the pan, leave it until it melts and becomes foamy before pouring in the beaten eggs—don't let it turn brown or it could spoil the flavor of your omelette.

**SERVES 1**

# BANANA BREAD

Making a loaf of banana bread is a good way to use up overripe bananas—the ones still in the fruit bowl that nobody wants to eat! Overripe bananas are wonderful and sweet and will give your banana bread a delicious flavor.

## INGREDIENTS

- 2 cups plain flour
- 2 tsp baking powder
- 1 tsp ground cinnamon
- 1 cup light soft brown sugar
- 3–4 overripe bananas
  2 eggs
- ¾ cup sunflower oil
- ⅓ cup raisins
- ½ cup chopped walnuts or
  pecans

### YOU WILL NEED

*Mixing bowl*          *Sieve*

*2 lb loaf pan, greased and lined with baking parchment*

*Wooden spoon*

*Standing blender, handheld mixer, or food processor*

*Wire cooling rack*

1 Preheat the oven to 350°F. Sift the flour, baking powder, and cinnamon into a mixing bowl and stir in the sugar.

2 Peel the bananas and cut them into chunks. Liquidize the bananas, eggs, and sunflower oil together and gradually beat into the dry ingredients.

### CHECK YOUR SKILLS

- p. 25 for using a blender
- p. 52 for beating ingredients together

*Easy peasy*

3 When all of the banana mixture has been added, stir in the raisins and walnuts or pecans.

4 Spoon the mixture into the loaf pan and bake for about 1 hour, or until a toothpick pushed into the center comes out clean.

5 Leave to cool in the pan for 30 minutes before turning out onto a wire rack and leaving to cool completely before peeling off the lining paper.

**QUICK TIP...**For a special treat, frost the banana bread with cream cheese icing. To make this, whisk together ½ cup of cream cheese, 4 tablespoons of softened butter, and 1 cup of sifted powdered sugar until smooth and creamy. Spread the frosting over the top and sides of the loaf with a palette knife.

**SERVES 8–10**

# MIXING, FOLDING & KNEADING

Almost all recipes involve mixing ingredients together but, depending on the recipe, this is done in different ways. Bread dough and muffin batters have their own separate techniques to make sure they rise properly and are deliciously light and airy when baked.

## EQUIPMENT NEEDED

### MUFFIN AND CUPCAKE TRAYS

These trays can be made of metal or silicone, and contain 6 or 12 cups. Use a tray with large cups for baking muffins, medium cups for baking cupcakes, and shallow cups for baking pastry tartlets.

### MIXING BOWL

A large bowl used for mixing ingredients for bread, muffins, cookie dough, and cake batter.

### CLING WRAP

A thin, transparent film made of plastic, used for covering bowls and dishes or wrapping food to keep out air.

## MIXING

Mixing is halfway between beating and folding. While beating involves a vigorous action and folding a very gentle one, mixing is combining ingredients by stirring them together with a metal or wooden spoon in a saucepan or bowl.

## FOLDING

When you've whisked lots of air into egg whites so they are light and foamy, the last thing you want is to beat all the air out again. To fold them gently into another mixture, use a large metal spoon or spatula, moving it in the shape of a large figure eight and stirring as lightly as possible. Continue to do this until everything is evenly mixed together.

## Technique 1: FOLDING MUFFIN MIXTURES

For light-as-air muffins, it's important not to beat the ingredients together too briskly. Simply fold them together until the dry ingredients are moistened by the wet ones.

1 Put the dry ingredients—flour, baking soda, and sometimes spices and sugar—into a mixing bowl (sifting them together so they are evenly mixed if the recipe calls for it).

2 Whisk the wet ingredients—eggs, melted butter or oil, and milk or another liquid—together in a measuring cup.

3 Make a well in the middle of the dry ingredients and pour the wet ingredients into it.

4 Gently fold the dry and wet ingredients together using a spatula, large spoon, or table fork until the dry ingredients are just moistened. Don't worry if there are lumps, these are fine.

5 Add the remaining ingredients, such as chopped nuts, dried fruits, grated carrots, fresh berries, mashed banana, or chocolate chips, and give the batter one more gentle stir to mix these ingredients in. Again, don't worry about any lumps.

6 Put paper muffin liners in the cups of a muffin tray—this helps the muffins keep their shape as they bake—and spoon the batter into them, filling the cases almost to the top. You can also bake the batter in the unlined cups, but spray them with a non-stick spray before you spoon the mixture in.

7 Bake the muffins according to your recipe, until risen and golden brown. Cool them for 5 minutes in the tray before lifting them out and placing them on a wire rack. Serve the muffins warm or leave to cool completely.

## Technique 2: KNEADING BREAD DOUGH

Few smells are as wonderful as homemade bread baking in the oven. All that's needed to make bread dough are four basic ingredients—flour, salt, liquid, and a rising agent—and these haven't changed since the time of the ancient Egyptians. Mix those ingredients together and follow a few simple rules. Your bread will rise to the occasion every time.

### MAIN INGREDIENTS OF BREAD

**FLOUR**
Use flour labeled "all purpose" or "bread flour." Using this kind of flour means that when the dough is kneaded, extra gluten is produced, giving the baked loaf a light, airy texture.

**YEAST**
This is used to make the dough rise. "Fast-action" or "easy-blend" yeast are the simplest to use and just need stirring into the flour.

**LIQUID**
This can be water or milk and, while it needs to be warm to encourage the dough to rise, it must not be hot or it will kill the yeast and your bread won't rise at all. The liquid needs to be around 98.4°F. To check if it is about the right temperature, dip a finger in and the liquid should feel warm.

**SALT**
A little salt helps the yeast work and gives your bread a better flavor.

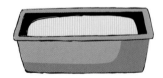

**1** Once you have made your bread dough (see recipe on page 60), it must be kneaded to work the gluten into the flour so the dough is smooth, elastic, and will rise properly. Put the dough on a lightly floured board and stretch and pull it vigorously to develop the gluten. Use the heel of one hand to push it away from you and then fold it back toward you to make a ball, turning the dough as you work. You'll need to do this for about 10 minutes to get the dough to a spongy texture.

**2** When you've finished kneading the dough, shape it into a ball and place it in a mixing bowl that's been lightly brushed with oil to stop the dough from sticking to it.

**3** Cover the bowl tightly with cling wrap—brush this with oil too if you think the dough will reach the top of the bowl when it rises—and leave the dough in a warm place, such as a sunny room, until it has doubled in size, which will take about 1¹/₂–2 hours.

**4** After the dough has risen, peel the cling wrap off the bowl and punch the dough back down with your fist. Knead it again on a lightly floured board for 1–2 minutes to disperse any air bubbles trapped in the dough.

**5** Shape the dough into a rectangle and place it in a greased loaf tin. Alternatively, shape the dough into a round shape, or cut it into small pieces, shaping into rolls, and place on a greased baking sheet.

**6** Cover the shaped dough loosely with cling wrap—oil the cling wrap lightly to stop the dough from sticking to it—and leave in a warm place for about 30–40 minutes until doubled in size again. The technical name for this second rising is called "proving," and it ensures the baked loaf has a more even texture than if it were only risen once.

# SEEDED BREAD ROLLS

## YOU WILL NEED

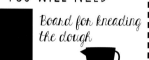

Board for kneading the dough

Measuring cup

Cling wrap

2 baking sheets, greased
Wire cooling rack

Mixing bowl

Spoon

Pastry brush

Knife

Measuring spoons

These rolls can be eaten on their own or with butter and jam, filled with your favorite sandwich ingredients, or served with a bowl of soup.

## INGREDIENTS

- ¾ cup all-purpose white bread flour, plus extra for kneading
- ¾ cup wholemeal bread flour
- 4 tsp sugar
- 1½ tsp fast-action dried yeast
- ½ tsp salt
- Generous ½ cup warm milk
- 3 tbsp butter, melted and cooled
- 1 egg, beaten
- sunflower or canola oil, for greasing the mixing bowl, cling wrap, and baking sheets
- 1 egg yolk beaten with 2 tbsp cold water, to glaze
- 1 tbsp sesame seeds
- 1 tbsp poppy seeds

## CHECK YOUR SKILLS

- p. 59 for kneading bread dough
- p. 42–43 for using the oven

**SERVES 10**

1 Mix the white and wholemeal bread flours together in a mixing bowl and stir in the sugar, yeast, and salt.

2 Make a well in the center of the dry ingredients and pour in the milk, butter, and egg. Stir with a spoon until evenly mixed and then press the dough together with your hands to make a ball.

3 Transfer the dough to a board lightly dusted with flour and knead by hand for 10 minutes until the dough is smooth and elastic.

4 Place it in a mixing bowl that has been greased by brushing with oil, cover the bowl with cling wrap, and leave the dough to rise in a warm place for 1½–2 hours, or until it has doubled in size.

5 Punch the dough down with your fist and knead it again on a board for another 5 minutes. Cut it into 10 equal-sized pieces and roll each piece into a ball between the palms of your hands. Press the tops down lightly with your fingers to flatten them a little.

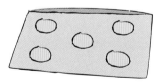

6 Divide the balls of dough between two greased baking sheets, spacing them far enough apart so they have room to rise. Cover with oiled cling wrap and leave to rise again for 30–40 minutes, or until doubled in size.

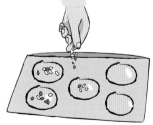

7 Preheat the oven to 400°F. Brush the rolls with the beaten egg yolk and sprinkle sesame seeds over half of them and poppy seeds over the other half.

8 Bake for about 20 minutes, or until golden brown, and the rolls sound hollow when tapped on the base. Slide onto a wire rack to cool.

**TRY THIS!**
Instead of shaping all of the dough into balls, roll some into thin sausages about 8 inches long and tie into knots.

# CHOCOLATE MOUSSE

Mmmm…this is the perfect dessert for chocoholics! This recipe uses a mix of milk and dark chocolate, but if you prefer a stronger flavor, use all dark chocolate.

## INGREDIENTS

- 4 tbsp butter
- 1 cup milk chocolate chips
- 1 cup dark chocolate chips
- 4 oz white mini marshmallows
- 4 tbsp milk
- 1¼ cup heavy cream

### YOU WILL NEED

Knife

Large heatproof bowl

Large metal spoon

Saucepan

Balloon whisk or handheld mixer

4 glasses or serving dishes

1 Cut up the butter into small pieces and put in a large heatproof bowl. Add the milk and dark chocolate chips, the mini marshmallows, and the milk.

2 Fill a saucepan one-third of the way with water, put it on the stove, and bring the water to a simmer. Turn the heat under the pan down to low and sit the bowl on top of the pan, making sure the bottom of the bowl doesn't touch the water.

### CHECK YOUR SKILLS

- p. 48 for melting chocolate
- p. 48 for using the stove
- p. 53 for whipping cream

3 In another bowl, whip the cream until it thickens and holds its shape.

4 Using a large metal spoon, fold the cream into the melted chocolate mixture until it is evenly mixed in and there are no white streaks of cream remaining.

### TRY THIS!

Decorate each mousse with a spoonful of whipped cream. Crumble a small chocolate flake and sprinkle that over the cream.

**SERVES 4**

5 Spoon the mixture into four glasses or serving dishes and chill in the fridge for 2–3 hours or until ready to serve.

**QUICK TIP...** If you can't find mini marshmallows, you can use large ones instead. Just snip them into small pieces with kitchen scissors first so they melt more easily.

# CARROT & PECAN MUFFINS

These muffins will get your day off to a great start! Have one for breakfast with a glass of fruit juice. You could also pack one for lunch or for a quick snack when you need an energy boost.

## YOU WILL NEED

12-cup muffin tray

12 paper muffin cases

Wire cooling rack

Skewer

Sieve

Mixing bowl

Measuring jug

Spatula, spoon, or table fork

## INGREDIENTS

- 2¼ cups plain flour
- 1½ tsp baking soda
- 1 tsp ground cinnamon
- ¾ cup sugar
- ⅔ cup sunflower or canola oil
- 3 large eggs
- 1 tsp vanilla extract
- ⅔ cup chopped pecans
- ⅔ cup raisins
- 1⅓ carrots (about 3½ carrots), grated
- 12 pecan halves

## CHECK YOUR SKILLS

- p. 59 for folding
- p. 13 for grating

MAKES 12

1 Preheat the oven to 350°F. Line a 12-cup muffin tray with paper muffin liners.

2 Sift the flour, baking soda, and cinnamon into a mixing bowl and stir in the sugar.

3 In a measuring cup, beat together the oil, eggs, and vanilla. Fold into the dry ingredients until just mixed in, using a spatula, spoon, or fork.

4 Stir in the pecans, raisins, and grated carrots.

5 Spoon the mixture into the muffin liners and top each with a pecan half. Bake for 20–25 minutes or until risen and golden. A toothpick pushed into the center of a muffin should come out clean.

**QUICK TIP...**Although the muffins are delicious eaten plain, you could also spread the tops of them with cream cheese icing (see Banana Bread recipe on page 57).

6 Cool in the tray for 15 minutes before carefully lifting the muffins out. Serve them warm or transfer to a wire rack to cool completely.

# GLOSSARY OF EQUIPMENT

**BOARDS** For cutting and chopping. Use separate boards for fruit and vegetables, fish, meat, and bread. Wash and dry thoroughly after use.

**CAKE AND TART PANS** These come in many different shapes and sizes, can be deep or shallow, and made of metal or silicone. Place silicone pans on a metal baking sheet before spooning in the batter.

**CASSEROLE** A large, deep ovenproof pan with straight sides and a tight-fitting lid, used for slow-cooked dishes such as stews.

**CLING WRAP** A thin transparent plastic film that "clings" to surfaces and itself. Used to cover bowls and dishes and to wrap food.

**COLANDER** A large bowl-shaped utensil with holes, used for draining foods such as pasta, vegetables, and rice.

**COOLING RACK** This allows air to move around baked goods as they cool to stop condensation from forming and making them soggy. Choose a rack with a narrow grid so that small items don't break or fall through.

**FISH SPATULA** A utensil with a long handle and a flat, blunt blade with holes. Used for turning food, particularly fish, and to lift and drain items from a pan when cooked.

**FOIL** A thin metal sheet of aluminum used for wrapping food in an airtight parcel to keep it fresh. Also used for lining grill pans and covering a dish in the oven to prevent the top from browning.

**GARLIC PRESS** A handy utensil for crushing garlic. Cloves are pushed through the press by squeezing two handles together, the skin remaining in the press while the clove is squeezed out as a purée.

**LADLE** A large spoon with a cup-shaped bowl and long handle used for serving sauces and soups.

**MEASURING JUG** A glass or plastic jug with marks for measuring liquid and dry ingredients.

**MEASURING SPOONS** A set of different sized spoons for measuring liquid and dry ingredients in quantities of 2.5 ml (½ tsp), 5 ml (1 tsp), 10 ml (1 dsp) and 15 ml (1 tbsp). Dry ingredients should be level with the top of the spoon.

**MIXING BOWL** Used for beating egg whites, whisking cream, and tossing salads, as well as mixing ingredients for cakes, cookies, and doughs.

**OVENPROOF COOKWARE** Any dish or tray made of ceramic, cast iron, silicone, or metal that is used for oven cooking. Examples include muffin trays, casseroles, and roasting tins. Always wear oven gloves when taking a dish out of the oven.

**PALETTE KNIFE** A knife with a long, flexible blade and rounded end that bends easily. The blade has no sharp edges and is used to spread frosting and cake fillings and for smoothing toppings, such as mashed potatoes.

**PAPER TOWELS** Food-safe absorbent paper used for lining plates to drain excess fat from fried foods and general kitchen jobs such as wiping utensils or mopping up spills.

**PASTRY BRUSH** Available with silicone or natural bristles, these food-safe brushes are used for tasks such as glazing pastry with beaten egg or milk and greasing tins. Wash well after use and dry before storing.

**ROLLING PIN** A long, heavy cylinder made of wood, marble, stainless steel, or plastic, used for flattening or rolling out dough.

**SCALES** For measuring quantities of ingredients needed for a recipe.

**SIEVE** Similar to a colander but with a finer mesh, used for sieving dry ingredients to remove lumps, sauces and soups to make them smooth, and soft fruits to remove seeds.

**SKEWERS** Made of wood or stainless steel. Small similar-sized pieces of raw food are threaded onto the skewers to make kebabs. Wooden ones need soaking for 30 minutes to prevent them burning.

**SPATULA** A thin flat tool made of wood, silicone, or metal with a broad, blunt blade. Used for mixing, spreading, turning food in a frying pan, and stir-frying.

**TONGS** Large, two-handled pinchers for turning burgers, sausages, and other meats on a grill, barbecue, or in a frying pan, lifting long pasta and corn cobs from boiling water, or for serving salads.

**WOODEN SPOON** A good alternative to a metal spoon (as it doesn't get hot) when cooking. Also, it does not scratch a pan with a non-stick coating. It is also used for beating cake batters or stirring ingredients together.

# INDEX